KV-013-237

The Concise Guide to

Gardening

Hints and Tips

igloobooks

Published in 2014
by Igloo Books Ltd
Cottage Farm
Sywell
NN6 0BJ
www.igloobooks.com

The measurements used are approximate.

HUN001 0214
2 4 6 8 10 9 7 5 3 1
ISBN 978-1-78197-072-0

Printed and manufactured in China

The Concise Guide to
Gardening
Hints and Tips

CONTENTS

INTRODUCTION

For those with a busy and demanding lifestyle, gardening can sometimes seem like a tedious activity, requiring consistent time and energy. However, as this concise guide aims to show, gardening can be an extremely pleasurable and often therapeutic hobby, even for the amateur gardener. Whilst it is true that a gardener must have effective awareness of factors such as timing, planning, climate and the changing seasons, this reference guide seeks to demonstrate that a rudimentary knowledge and a real passion for horticulture is all the true gardener really needs. This book has something to offer for both seasoned and budding gardeners hoping to develop a new, green-fingered hobby.

The clearly defined sections are useful for those new to gardening and wanting to dip their fingers into a particular area, whether you want to set up a plot or green house, to nurture fruit and vegetables or simply sow sunflower seeds. For the more advanced gardener or to those who pursue the hobby devotedly all year round, there is valuable seasonal advice to help plan ahead and to ensure that the garden is kept under flourishing conditions. There is even a unique assortment of 'Projects' for those wishing to get stuck into more substantial endeavours.

Every garden should be an extension of the home; a place to relax, to entertain, to play and to enjoy your hobbies. Whether you have a small yard or acres of grassy land, you can make your garden stunning with this inspirational book.

FRUIT AND VEGETABLES

PLAN YOUR VEG PATCH

Plan ahead to make sure you get what you want from your plot.

Keeping a veg plot productive and looking good all year round requires planning. And because winter is a quiet time (digging is done, not much to sow, and weed growth is slow), it's a great time to plan ahead. Best of all, it can be done indoors!

But to achieve a year-round productive and aesthetically pleasing plot, there are many things to consider. Where do you start? Hopefully the sequence of events below will set you on the right path.

DO YOU CURRENTLY HAVE A VEG PLOT?

You have a plot where you've grown veg for one or more years. To avoid a disease build-up, don't to grow the same crops on the same part of the plot over succeeding years.

Do you follow a crop rotation plan?

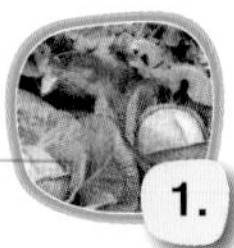

Group separately potatoes, peas and beans, brassicas and root crops, and divide the plot into four distinct growing areas. Each veg group is moved one area forward each year: brassicas (cabbages, cauliflowers, broccoli, sprouts and swedes) follow peas and beans; peas and beans follow root crops; root crops follow potatoes; potatoes follow brassicas.

You have a garden, but have never grown vegetables before - or you may have just taken over an allotment for the first time.

Have you marked out the ground?

If not already done, you'll need to measure off and mark out the area, and then dig it over. Don't delay in doing this, particularly if your soil is clay (the winter frosts break up the clods making the soil much easier to work). Choose a day when the ground is neither waterlogged nor frosted. Dig the plot, two spade blades deep if possible, working in rows. Add well-rotted manure or compost at all levels. If converting lawn, remove the top couple of inches and stack the turf in a pile to rot down.

Have you considered raised beds?

These can be made yourself, or are available by mail order and from some garden centres. They have rigid sides so that you can build up a depth of soil within them. This makes the bed easier to maintain if you find it difficult to stoop, or want to grow deep root crops.

GET GREENHOUSE TOMS ON THE GO

SOWING TOMATOES EARLY WILL GIVE YOU THE BEST CHANCE OF A BUMPER CROP.

Who knows what the weather will hold this year, but we can all boost our cropping potential with some early seed sowing. By giving tomatoes the longest growing season possible, you greatly increase the chances of good yields of succulent, ripe fruit. Started in a heated propagator, plants can be placed in the greenhouse in early spring to catch sunshine.

You don't need a lot of space to sow – a 3in (7.5cm) pot will yield multiple seedlings.

Winter light levels can lead to stretched plants but my tips below will help overcome this.

QUICK TIP

Make a second sowing of tomato seed in early spring for growing on in the outdoor vegetable patch.

PRODUCING THE BEST PLANTS

Put seedlings into grow tubes for deep root development as soon as the first true leaves appeared.

Low light in winter can lead to plants stretching; prevent this by keeping plants on a warm, south-facing windowsill. But even here, stretching can occur. Use kitchen foil to create a reflective backing to raise light intensity around your plants, or try a reflective 'space blanket'. These are cheap to buy at camping/sport shops and will reflect sunlight and warmth back to your seedlings.

Once roots show through the grow tubes set the plants in large pots of multipurpose compost.

SOMETHING OLD, SOMETHING NEW...

We all have our favourite types of tomato, and you should continue to grow these year to year. But with so many to choose from, do try at least one new variety each year.

STEP BY STEP

Take a small seed tray or a 3in (7.5cm) pot and fill with seed and cuttings compost (break up any lumps and bumps first). Tap down to settle, and level to create an even sowing surface.

Open your chosen seed packet and evenly tap a dozen or so seeds across the surface of the compost. Do not allow seeds to sit so close to each other that root damage occurs to one when pricking out another.

Cover with a thin layer of compost or vermiculite and label the pot. Place in a heated propagator, or cover with a clear plastic bag, and place on a warm windowsill. Uncover when seedlings appear.

SOWING SWEET PEAS

Sow a batch of sweet peas mid-late winter as a back-up to autumn-sown seedlings.

Sweet peas are so easy to grow; perfect if you are new to gardening.

Being hardy annuals they can cope with cold, but a little protection helps.

Seeds sown in autumn and again in winter, produce plants ready to flower from early summer, compared to a spring sowing, which often lags well behind.

A mid-winter sowing also acts as a back-up, in case autumn seedlings suffer from an unexpected disease or pest problem. Lack of air flow in the greenhouse in winter can lead to fungal infection, and aphids can survive the winter under glass.

Sowing in mid-winter is also a great excuse to garden in the warmth of the home or greenhouse.

There are so many gorgeous varieties of sweet pea to choose from that you can use a mid-winter sowing as an excuse to grow those you didn't have room for in autumn.

VARIETIES TO TRY

- 'Blue Ripple': beautiful shade of blue and highly scented.
- 'Annual Species Mixed' Bright rainbow colours and less frilly petals.
- 'Lady Turral': Strong-scented magenta and lilac blooms.
- 'Summer sizzler': Shades of orange and red with a lovely fragrance.

SOWING SWEET PEAS

Sweet peas set long roots and need plenty of depth to grow before planting out in spring. Sow in deep root trainers or toilet rolls, one seed per cell pushed down to a depth of 1in (2.5cm). Or set three seeds in 3in (7.5cm) pots. Use seed compost and give some gentle heat to aid germination in severe cold weather, but stop artificial heat once the seeds have germinated.

ONGOING CARE

As soon as the majority of seeds have sprouted, move the batch to a cold frame or cold greenhouse – any extra heat will cause the plants to stretch. Keep just moist. Once seedlings reach around 4in (10cm), or have put on three or so leaf sets, pinch out the growing tips to encourage multiple branching. If severe frost is forecast, cover with newspaper to protect the soft growth.

POTTING ON

Your sweet pea seedlings may need potting on before planting out if spring weather is not suitable. Look for roots coming through the bottom of root trainers or pots. The compost will also have run out of nutrients to promote growth after a couple of months. Pot on in deep pots filled with multipurpose compost to allow continued unrestricted root growth. Keep well watered.

GET CHILLIES ON THE GO

For the biggest plants and best harvests.

SPEEDY CHILLIES

1. Add warm water to your coir pellets and allow to soak, fluff up and bulk out. Pour away excess water so seeds do not become saturated

2. Use a dibber to create small sowing holes and set one or two seeds in place.

3. Pinch the compost closed over the seed and cover with a clear lid. Set on a windowsill and keep moist. Wipe condensation from the lid, removing lid fully once seedlings emerge.

Chillies in all their different shapes, sizes and heat levels are a great annual plant to grow in the greenhouse.

To get the best plants in mid-winter start early. Light levels aren't perfect at this time, but if the seedlings become leggy you can pinch them out at 6in (15cm) tall to encourage side branching and a bushier growth habit as the plant develops.

There are many ways to sow chillies. At a temperature of 18°C (64°F) upwards you'll soon have seedlings to tend, and as early as summer you could be adding your own heat to your favourite curries and spicy dishes.

PLANTING ASPARAGUS

Planting asparagus crowns is easy, but you need patience to grow them.

Asparagus crowns do well in the warmer soil of a raised bed, but they need plenty of space to mature and crop well in future years.

If there is one veg that is worth growing to save you money, it's asparagus, but it does require patience. You mustn't harvest them for two years after planting, so they build up energy to produce good spears in following years.

Early spring is the best time to plant dormant crowns. Asparagus does best in well-drained soil, and just requires weeding, mulching and watering to grow a good crop. Most varieties are male plants, as these produce a tastier crop.

For planting, pick a sunny site, which has a neutral pH, somewhere between 6.5 and 7. Remove all weeds and dig in well rotted-manure or compost. Then follow the guide below.

VEGETABLES

SOW SOME VEG SEEDS OUTDOORS UNDER CLOCHES NOW

Sow some quick maturing veg for an early crop, and give others that need a long growing season an early start. But to ensure good germination and avoid frost damage they'll need the protection of cloches.

Early sowings often need less care as they tend to be ready to crop before many pests and diseases become a problem.

The type of cloche you use doesn't matter, as long as it maintains soil temperature, and allows a good level of light to reach the seeds.

Warm up the soil a couple of weeks beforehand by placing the cloches over the site where the seeds are to be sown. Remember to keep the soil watered underneath in very dry weather. Veg that can be sown now are listed right. Northern regions may need to wait a few more weeks.

On sunny days remove cloches to harden up the seedlings, but take care to replace these at night until frosts pass.

SEEDS TO GET OFF TO AN EARLY START

- Asparagus peas
- Beetroot
- Peas
- Spring onions
- Carrots
- Lettuce
- Broad beans
- Summer cabbage
- Celeriac
- Radishes
- Chicory

RASPBERRY MAINTENANCE

It's time to plant new canes, and also sort out established autumn croppers.

There are two types of raspberry – autumn croppers and summer croppers. Both are easy to grow, but stick to the autumn types to spread your fruit harvest. In summer you might have strawberries to pick, so you won't mind waiting for the raspberries.

Handily, the autumn types fruit on new canes produced in the same year, making pruning easy and removing the need for supports.

To get a bumper crop from your autumn raspberries, prune, feed and replant now. Here's how...

Early spring is the best time to prune autumn raspberries. With the bed cleared, feed and mulch the crowns. You can also plant new canes.

1.

Autumn raspberries simply need cutting down to ground level at the end of winter. If canes are crowded in summer, you can thin them.

2.

Plant new canes. Dig a hole large enough to add compost, spread out the roots and set the cane at the same level as it was in the pot.

3.

To get early growth off to the best start, apply a topdressing of balanced fertiliser or fish blood and bone.

4.

To keep weeds down, retain moisture and add further goodness to the soil, apply 3in (7.5cm) of well-rotted manure or compost.

BLUEBERRY CONTAINERS

For some gardeners, blueberry growing is only really successful in pots.

A lot of claims are made about the 'superfruit' on a blueberry bush: high nutrient and vitamin levels, high in antioxidants, anti-cancer properties… the list goes on. Fruiting aside, blueberries make a decorative addition to the garden, particularly in autumn when the leaves turn from green through shades of red, purple and yellow. And the bell-like flowers make a strong statement in spring too.

However, if your soil is neutral to alkaline you won't have much success with these acid-loving plants. If you have heavy clay, or limey soil, adjusting its acidity can be difficult, and the prepared area can quickly lose the acidity you add to it as well. So your best chance of growing blueberries is to set them in pots filled with ericaceous compost.

Early spring is the best month to establish blueberries in pots, giving them a full season of growth before facing up to a cold winter outside.

QUICK TIP

Get the most from your ericaceous pots: underplant blueberries with acid-loving cranberries.

TIPS FOR SUCCESS

- No matter when you buy your blueberry plant, potting up is best done in early spring.
- Apply an ericaceous feed each April to help with fruit development.
- Use rain water when possible. Tap water contains lime which will alter the pH level of the compost over time.
- Blueberries fruit on last year's growth, and older. No pruning is needed in the first three years, although removing stem tips on plants with few side shoots should encourage bushier growth early on.
- Place netting over plants as fruit ripens, to prevent losing it to hungry birds.

POTTING GUIDE

- Blueberries prefer an annual repotting. They take around eight years to mature, and should go into slightly larger pots each year until you reach an eventual pot diameter of 3ft (90cm).
- Each spring choose a weather-proof pot a few inches wider than the existing pot.
- Line the base with an inch or so of grit/gravel for drainage.
- Add a few inches of ericaceous compost to the bottom, so that when placed, the top of the root ball is just below the pot rim.
- Pack around the rootball with more compost, firming down as you go.
- Apply a topdressing of grit/gravel to help retain moisture and prevent weed growth.
- Water to settle in, but only use rain water.

GIVE YOUR BERRIES A BOOST

Blueberries don't need a pollinating partner to fruit, so if you're short on space just plant one. However, grow two or more plants close to each other and both will crop heavier than if stood alone. All varieties flower around the same time, but fruits ripen at different times according to variety.

GROWING STRAWBERRIES

Simple steps to planting and growing delicious strawberries.

Strawberries are one of the most popular fruits to grow, and early spring is a great time to get them started. There are three main types: alpine, (small in size), summer fruiting and ever bearers that produce fruit through summer and early autumn.

If possible, grow a few of each for a regular supply of fruit over the summer and into early autumn.

Strawberries can either be grown from seed, or bought as cold stored runners (generally available from through spring and summer), or open-ground runners. Young plants grown in pots are widely available from garden centres.

To prepare a planting site outdoors, dig well-rotted organic garden compost or manure into the soil a few weeks before planting.

If you choose to grow strawberries from seed, you'll have to wait a little longer for fruits, but the upside is the number of plants you will be able to grow at little cost.

STEP BY STEP

Sowing alpine strawberry seeds

1.

Fill a seed tray with seed compost. Tap to settle and level the compost then sieve a thin layer on top of this to create fine layer on the surface for the seed to bed into.

2.

Water the compost with a fine rose watering can using tap water. Sow the seeds on the top of the compost. Most alpine strawberry seeds need light to germinate so leave uncovered.

3.

Place the seeds in a greenhouse or cold frame at a temperature of 15°c (59°F), or place in a heated propagator. Transplant the seedlings into small pots when large enough to handle.

Established strawberry plants need a tidy up, a feed high in potash to increase their fruit yields and a mulch with some fresh compost.

Six strawberry varieties to try:

- 'Florence'
- 'Honeoye'
- 'Marshmello'
- 'Cambridge'
- 'Elsanta'
- 'Mignonette'

ESTABLISHED PLANTS

If you already have strawberries growing in your garden, give them some attention. Remove all brown and dead leaves and any runners that have rooted over winter, which are not needed. If keeping some, cut the stem from the parent plant to separate them. Add a layer of well-rotted manure or compost mulch to enrich the soil.

GROWING IN CONTAINERS

Strawberries do well in pots, baskets or growing bags. They do need adequate space to grow – too many plants crammed in a pot will result in fewer fruits.

For a 12in pot or basket, use three strawberry plants. Use good potting compost enriched with well rotted manure. Check compost daily and keep watered so they do not dry out.

STRAWBERRY BLACK EYE

At this time of year the main problem with early varieties is a condition called strawberry black eye. The parts of the flower that produce the fruit become black due to frost damage, resulting in no fruit.

Protect early flowers from frost by covering with fleece or a cloche. Avoid planting early strawberries in exposed areas.

POLLINATING EARLY FLOWERS

For an early crop of fruit, grow some in baskets and containers in the greenhouse, or cold frame.

At this time of year, in poor weather, the insect population, which aids pollination of the flowers, may be low. To ensure the flowers set fruit, use a small paintbrush to transfer pollen between them.

PEAS IN QUEUES

Try sowing early peas in lengths of gutter pipe filled with compost.

Guttering can become the perfect home for your first sowings of early peas in the greenhouse.

Saw the guttering into three lengths, to match the width of your raised beds. Then drill drainage holes along the bases and block the ends by taping across some sturdy black plastic. Fill each length to just below the edge with multipurpose compost and plant two staggered rows of peas 2in (5cm) apart. Push down about 1in (2.5cm) deep. After watering, lift up into position on the greenhouse staging.

You might be well advised to set traps if rodents are a problem.

Choose early pea cultivars as they're quicker to crop and make shorter, easily supported plants.

Transplanting is tricky as it's easy to damage the young plant roots.

1.

Fill lengths of gutter with compost

Sow seeds 2in (5cm) apart in rows

3.

Slide out young plants into the soil

NOTES:

GREENHOUSE TOMATOES

How to succeed with tomatoes in growing bags under cover this year.

QUICK TIP

Before planting your tomatoes, shake the compost in the growing bag to loosen and get rid of any lumps.

If you have a greenhouse – or a conservatory you don't mind filling with greenery – you can now plant tomatoes into growing bags. They should become nicely established and actively growing before plants destined for outdoor cultivation are even a few inches high!

Bags are so useful because they are convenient, self-contained and space-saving. Tomatoes are particularly suited to them. The compost within (unless the bag is labelled as being formulated specifically for leafy crops, potatoes, herbs or flowers) is generally tailored to fruiting plants, such as tomatoes.

The main downside to growing bags is that they contain a limited amount of compost, meaning that they dry out relatively quickly compared to plants growing in the garden soil. However, there are several ways to prevent this happening.

First you could grow just two plants per bag rather than the recommended three. Or you could stand the bag on its side (propped so it stays upright), which then gives a greater depth of soil for the roots to grow in. You can also set up an irrigation system to deliver a controlled amount of water throughout the day, so they do not dry out if you are away.

Alternatively, plant the young tomato plants in a bottomless flowerpot set on the surface of the growing bag compost. This gives a greater volume of compost for the roots to grow in and establish. It also results in less watering and feeding as the bags hold moisture better. See below to find out how to do it.

THE FEEDING REGIME

To get the best crop of tomatoes you need to feed the plants properly – fail to feed and you'll fail to achieve any kind of a decent yield later in the year.

It's a good idea to feed your plants weekly with a weak solution of organic seaweed fertiliser – do this from the time the seedlings have been potted up until the first flowers have set. At this point change the weekly feed to a high-potash tomato fertiliser. In all cases, combining these feeds with watering means hardly any extra time and effort is required.

STEP BY STEP

'Bottomless pot' tomatoes in growbags

1.

With a sharp knife, cut a round hole in the bag. Most bags house three plants, but cropping can sometimes be better with just two.

2.

For each plant, take a 7in (17.5cm) plastic pot and remove some of the base. Push this into the hole you have created in the bag.

3.

Place multi-purpose compost in the pot so that it merges with the compost in the bag, and then plant your tomato plant into it.

4.

Place multipurpose compost in Insert a supporting cane into the pot (but don't damage the roots); tie the tomato plant to it, and finally water the plant in.

NOTES:

PLANTING POTATOES

Whatever the difficulties, potatoes are well worth growing.

Potatoes grow well in Scotland. The cool, rarely dry summers allow the tubers to swell without the need for endless irrigation, which, combined with their abundant, weed-suppressing foliage, makes them an easy, productive crop most years.

FRESHLY CULTIVATED

Potatoes are a good way to improve freshly cultivated ground.

There is little point planting potatoes into cold, wet soil, but once conditions have improved and the ground has begun to warm up, dig trenches to almost a spade's depth, about 16in (40cm) apart and fill with a thick layer of compost. Nestle the chitted tubers into this soft bed around 14in (35cm) apart, with their tops 2in (5cm) below the soil surface, and let the soil gently tumble in around them without breaking the delicate shoots. Arrange rows of taller veg from north to south on a north-facing slope if possible, to allow the plants plenty of sunlight.

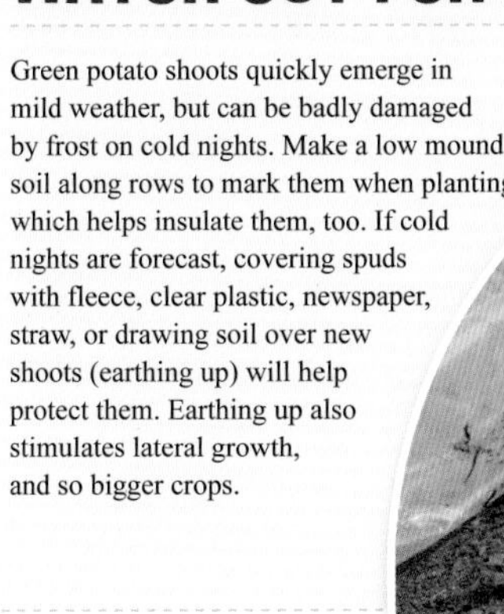

WATCH OUT FOR FROST

Green potato shoots quickly emerge in mild weather, but can be badly damaged by frost on cold nights. Make a low mound of soil along rows to mark them when planting, which helps insulate them, too. If cold nights are forecast, covering spuds with fleece, clear plastic, newspaper, straw, or drawing soil over new shoots (earthing up) will help protect them. Earthing up also stimulates lateral growth, and so bigger crops.

MAKING THE MOST OF HERBS

Tasty and attractive, herbs do well in baskets, containers and borders.

Herbs can be annual, biennial or perennial. They prefer to grow in a sunny position with well-drained soil. Take into account when choosing a site that it needs to be easily accessible so you can maintain and harvest your herbs. They grow well in containers, and are best sited near to the kitchen door for easy picking when required for use in cooking.

In early spring, hardy annual and perennial herbs can be sown or planted outside in the ground. Late spring is best for tender herbs, when the risk of frosts has passed.

If planting in containers, have one pot with hardy varieties in it, and another with the tender annuals such as basil. Herbs prefer a deep pot, such as a 'Long Tom', which lets them grow deep roots.

Some herbs can also be propagated by division, root cuttings or seed.

QUICK TIP

Sow dill and bronze fennel directly outdoors to add textured foliage to mixed flower borders.

STEP BY STEP PLANTING IN CONTAINERS

1. Use a container deep enough for good root growth. Fill two thirds of the pot with multipurpose compost with added grit.

2. Position the herbs in the pot to see how they look; plant in odd numbers if possible. Ensure you allow room for growth between them.

3. Plant the herbs, and fill around them with compost. Leave a gap of 1in (2.5cm) between compost and the rim of the pot for watering.

PLANTING IN THE GROUND

Harden off young herb plants before setting them out in a weed-free, well-drained soil. Gently push the plant out of its pot, handling it by its leaves or rootball, not the stem as this can be easily damaged. Plant into a hole, so the top of the rootball is at or just below the surface. Gently firm in, and water. Keep watering, especially in dry spells until plants are established.

WAYS TO PROPAGATE HERBS IN SPRING

MOUND LAYERING

Some herbs, such as sage and thyme, become woody over a few years and this can decrease their life span and the ability to produce new growth. It's easy to form new plants from the parent by 'mound layering' them:

- Mix multipurpose compost 50:50 with sand.
- Mound up the mixed compost around the herb, so the tips of the plant are just showing.
- Water regularly and replace any compost that washes away.
- Roots should form along the stems by late summer; cut these growths from the parent plant and pot up.
- Discard the old plant.

DIVIDING

Chives, mint, lemon balm, oregano (and marjoram) can be divided in spring, for extra plants.

- Lift the root ball of the mother plant from the ground or pot.
- If the plant is small, gently pull it apart, ensuring there are plenty of roots on each section.
- Medium-sized plants can be divided by simply cutting through the middle using a clean knife.
- With large herbs, insert two garden forks back to back and prise apart.
- Plant or pot up the new sections immediately, and water well.

SOWING HARDY HERBS

Many herbs can be grown successfully from seed. Sow the hardy herbs (such as chives, coriander and mint) in winter. Later, when the weather is warmer, sow tender herbs such as basil and French tarragon.

- Fill either pots or module trays with seed compost.
- Tap to settle the compost, then water and allow to drain.
- Sprinkle the seed thinly and evenly on the top of the compost.
- Some herbs need a fine layer of sieved compost over them, while some do not; check the instructions on the seed packet.
- Place hardy herb seeds in a coldframe or unheated greenhouse; tender varieties should be kept on a warm windowsill.

ROOT CUTTINGS OF MINT

Mint grows well from 'root cuttings' taken in spring.

- Remove the mint plant from its container, or lift a section of root from the ground. Wash the roots with water.
- Fill a pot with multipurpose compost with added grit to aid drainage and root formation.
- Find a long root of pencil thickness and remove from the plant with secateurs.
- Cuttings need planting the right way up, so cut the top straight and the base on a slanted. Or just lay the cuttings flat on compost!
- Cut the root into sections 2-4in (5-10cm) long. Insert each piece into the compost, so that its top is just below the surface. Then water.
- Place in a coldframe or unheated greenhouse.

LETTUCE GET GOING

It's safe to sow and plant out salad leaves as the weather warms up.

It's a good idea to sow a few hearting lettuces in the greenhouse in early spring to harden off and plant out now as spring edging for vegetable beds. This method gives good germination, eliminates the need for thinning and delays slug attacks until the plants are a decent size.

These big heads of lettuce are great when you need a lot but when you just want a few leaves for lunch, cut-and-come-again salads come into their own. They are a quick, simple and convenient way to grow a diverse range of baby leaves of lettuce, salad rocket, oriental mustard and mizuna.

Sow lettuce seeds in modules under glass.

SOW THINLY

Sow seed thinly (about ½in/1cm apart) in drills, but cut-and-come-again salads work well sown in wide bands, blocks and containers too.

Plants usually reach the baby leaf stage in about six weeks, when they can be harvested. Cut above the growing point for a second flush of leaves. On fertile soil, and kept well watered, they can produce three or four crops.

The pale, bitter leaves of Witloof chicory are worth buying. Sow several rows, about 12in (30cm) apart, in raised beds.

Harden off young plants to set out in the soil.

HOME-GROWN CHRISTMAS VEG

Plan ahead and grow your favourite winter veg for the festive season.

Look for winter cropping varieties, and those that will grow fast. There are parsnips that if sown in summer will still be a reasonable size for Christmas, and taste just as sweet. Plug plants can be a good deal if you're just growing a few plants.

If you are leaving parsnips and other edibles in the ground, cover the soil a few days before lifting, with plastic sheeting or cloches, in case the ground freezes.

QUICK TIP

When seedlings are big enough to handle, thin out to the correct spacing to ensure they have room to grow.

BRUSSELS SPROUTS

Brussels sprouts should be sown in spring as they are slow growing, but there are many varieties available as plug plants from garden centres. Plant the plugs in moist, fertile soil, with a spacing of about 2.5ft (75cm) between them. Feed in late summer with chicken manure pellets, at the rate of 5oz (150g) per sqm, as they require plenty of nitrogen to grow.

To avoid wind damage to the stem in autumn, support the plants by staking them with canes and mounding soil around the base.

PLUG PLANTS

Many of the vegetables you will want to grow as part of your Christmas dinner will be widely available as plug plants. These are great if you missed the sowing window or don't have space for trays of seedlings.

When you get them home, water them well before planting out. They may need to be potted on into a slightly larger container until they have a better root system.

CARROTS

Choose a maincrop variety such as 'Autumn King'. For growing in containers try 'Chantenay'.

To sow, create a fine, level tilth with a rake and water the soil. Place a bamboo cane on its side into the soil to create a thin drill. Sow the seeds and lightly cover with the soil. Keep well watered.

PARSNIPS

Parsnips can be sown in summer for a crop of baby roots in time for Christmas. On raked, stone-free soil, make a drill. Sow three seeds at 6in (15cm) intervals, cover with a sprinkling of soil and water well. If more than one seed germinates per grouping, thin these down to the strongest seedling.

CABBAGE

Winter cabbages are a hardy group that will grow well in winter. Sow into a modular tray and thin out when large enough to handle. Pot on into 3in (7cm) pots. Transplant once new growth is seen into their final position, planting deeply to just under their first leaves.

POTATOES

Potatoes can be grown in containers or open soil for a Christmas crop. The tubers do not need chitting. Cold-stored seed tubers are available from mid-summer. You can plant those bought earlier in the year, but not those harvested from this season – they need to have a dormant period. From autumn, cover potatoes outdoors with cloches and put pot grown spuds undercover to protect from frosts.

SWEDE

Swede can be sown up to eary summer. Sow in shallow drills 1/2 in (1cm) deep. When large enough to handle, thin out seedlings to 6in (15cm) apart. The variety 'Magres' is very hardy and the foliage is resistant to mildew.

HERBS

Herbs have many uses at Christmas time. They are best placed in a sheltered spot away from cold winds. Basil will grow indoors from a sowing as late as mid-summer. Mint leaves can be frozen before they die down. Herbs like a deep pot filled with well-drained gritty soil.

LEEKS

Leeks are best grown in open ground or deep raised beds. To grow them on, make holes 6in (15cm) deep in rows 12in (30cm) apart. Drop the plants into the hole and water in to allow the roots to settle. There is no need to backfill the holes with soil.

Keep problems at bay

- Use collars on brassicas to prevent cabbage root fly.
- Erect fleece around carrots to prevent carrot root fly.
- Net brassicas from pigeons and cabbage white butterfly using a fine netting mesh.
- Root vegetables can split if a dry summer is followed by a wet autumn. Water regularly to prevent this.
- Keep an eye out for slugs and snails and get rid of them.

CRANBERRIES

It wouldn't be a Christmas lunch without cranberries. These plants need an acidic, boggy soil, so are best grown in containers with ericaceous compost. Choose the American varieties of *Vaccinium macrocarpon* and opt for a bush more than two years old if you want it to crop this autumn.

Keep well watered during the summer so they do not dry out, otherwise they may drop their fruits. Once ripe, they are best left on cut vines, but they can also be frozen.

RHUBARB, RHUBARB!

Spring/summer is the rhubarb pulling season, but don't overdo it.

At any time you should leave three to four mature leaves on the plant; these will help sustain the plant and keep it growing.

Rhubarb is one of the few perennial vegetables (along with, amongst others, globe artichoke and asparagus). This makes it a valuable and cost-effective addition to the kitchen garden. Harvesting correctly will ensure plants lasts for years.

Crop rhubarb according to its age. Don't pull any stalks in the first year as this will weaken it. Instead, allow plants to establish strong root systems; leave the stalks and leaves intact to die down at the end of the season.

In the second season, harvest only for a couple of weeks, just selecting the stalks that are large enough. Allow plenty to remain on the plant. More generous harvesting can then take place from the third year.

Rhubarb stalks are ready to pull when they are between ½ in (1.5cm) and 2in (2.5cm) wide. They should be quite firm, and well coloured.

It is important to pull a stalk properly. Never cut it off as this will not produce vigorous new healthy re-growth.

Hold the stalk as close as possible to its base. Pull gently, whilst twisting, to ensure it comes away neatly. This invigorates the roots to produce more stems.

Never leave any bits of broken stem on the plant as these can introduce infections, rotting the crown.

Cut off any flowering stalks when they appear.

Stop harvesting once all of the stalks become thin, about two months or so after you started. If you continue to harvest, expect far fewer stalks the following year.

BROAD BEANS

Sow overwintering broad beans in late autumn for an early crop of pods the following summer.

The idea of sowing or planting any crops late in the year is to reap an early harvest in spring or early summer. The young plants spend the autumn and winter establishing a good root system, and so get away to a better start as the weather warms up again. With not much else growing at this time, broad beans are a worthwhile crop over the winter, in containers or in the soil.

To succeed you need to sow hardy broad beans (some are tender varieties) – there are several on offer nowadays but the old, reliable standard overwintering variety is 'Aquadulce'. This is quite tall growing, reaching 3ft (90cm) or more, so it needs a good sized container – a large 30litre pot or a veg growing bag.

To get the seeds off to a good start, sow into root trainers or large cell trays filled with multipurpose compost. Set one seed per cell, slightly below the surface, water well and pop it somewhere warm and bright – a windowsill, or a cold frame will do. Germination is generally very reliable, but watch out for mice – they love pinching the seeds!

Fill your bag and pot with recycled compost refreshed with plenty of well rotted horse manure and some blood, fish and bone fertiliser. Fresh multipurpose compost on its own is fine to use but costly.

Plant the young beans roughly 8in (20cm) apart each way, and arrange canes together with string to support plants as they grow. Young plants should be in the ground by late autumn. Protect plants with fleece if the weather is very cold or snowy. Otherwise they should need little attention.

Sow seeds now in root trainers filled with multipurpose compost

When 6in (15cm) tall, set plants in container 8in (20cm) apart

Water well, provide supports for plants, and protect from cats!

Serious growth will take off in spring, and in a good year you should get pickings by the end of spring. Watch out for blackfly on plant tips as the weather warms – spray with a contact organic insecticide. Pick beans when you can see the swellings along the pods.

Harvested small the beans are firm, tender and sweet, but if you let them go they can get very big – at this point the beans inside the pods develop a thick skin, and the flesh takes on a powdery texture. Blanch and skin each bean before eating.

You can sow other varieties to plant in spring for summer harvest, but there are more rewarding crops than these to be had from the limited space container growing allows.

PLANTING APPLES

Winter is the perfect time to plant apples, but don't just buy one on impulse.

This fan tree will produce fruit without crowding the border in front.

A happy apple tree can last a life time in the garden, but it pays to take a few simple things into consideration before rushing out to buy a new tree.

There are dozens of varieties to choose from (both eaters and cookers), but firstly, where will you site it? Do you want to train it against a wall or have it free-standing? What size do you want it to reach? You may need more than one tree for pollination, so which pollination group will you choose from to ensure good fruit set each year?

Then of course you'll have to decide between a bare-root or container-grown tree. Both can be planted through winter. Container plants are readily

STEP BY STEP Setting out container-grown apple trees

1.

Dig a hole twice the size of the tree's pot, and slightly deeper. Fill the extra depth with compost and fish, blood and bone, and mix in.

2.

Set the rootball in place, first teasing out any densely matted roots. Set a cane across the top to check it is level with the surrounding soil.

3.

Loosen the stake, drive it into the soil for anchorage, re-tie it, then fill around roots with a soil, compost and fertiliser mix. Press it down with your heel.

APPLES IN POTS

Many types of apple will grow well in a large patio or balcony pot. Buy trees grafted on to dwarfing rootstocks. The pot size needs to have a diameter ideally of 12-15in (30-38cm).

Wooden tubs are recommended for growing fruit (of all kinds) as they help insulate roots through winter. Terracotta pots can crack in winter frosts and dry quickly in summer heat. To plant, use a recommended tree compost, and make sure that the tree is well staked.

available at the garden centre and can be set out at any time, although the dormant season is still the preferred time to plant. The main deciding factor between bare-root and pot-grown is price. Bare-root trees are a much cheaper way of adding fruit trees to the garden. Just be sure to dig out a planting hole large enough to fan out the roots without cramming them in. If needed, trim one or two of the longest roots – but don't remove too many of them.

Choose a mild day to plant, when the soil is neither frozen or waterlogged. The steps below will get container-trees off to the best of starts.

QUICK TIP

The only difference between cooking and eating (dessert) apples is that the former are too tart or sharp to eat raw.

Shapes and rootstocks

- Free-standing: Unrestricted trees grown either as bush, half-standard or standard, with the latter being the largest. With a bush tree there should always be a clear stem of at least 30in (75cm) before the branches start. This increases to 4.5ft (1.35m) for half-standards, and 6ft (1.8m) for standards.

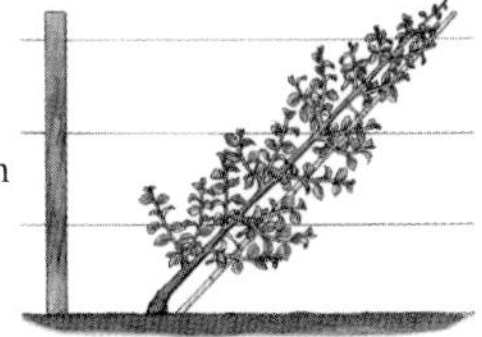

- Cordons: Restricted forms grown as a single stem, often trained at a 45° angle, and closely spaced to grow several trees in a small area. They flourish on post and wire supports, walls and fences. Double stemmed, U-shaped cordons are also widely available.

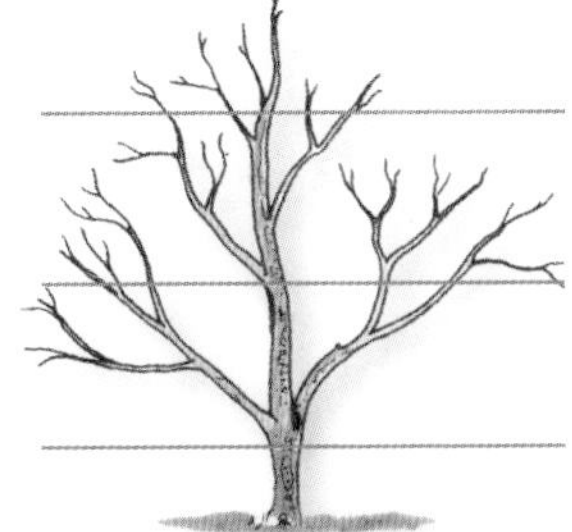

- Fans: Here, the apple tree's branches are trained and pruned to radiate out on either side of the central stem, and are attached to wires. Fans can be trained on free-standing posts and wires, or a fence or wall. This is a great space-saver for small gardens.

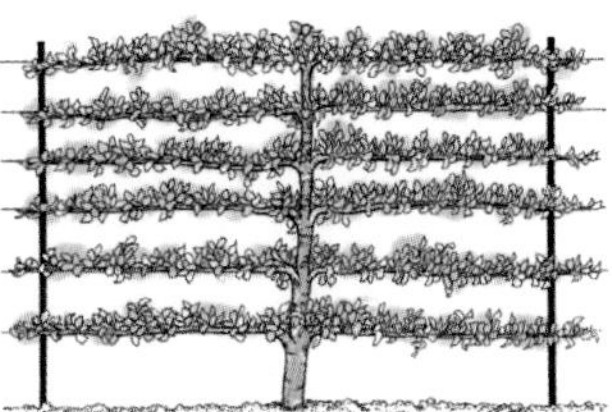

- Step-overs: This could be called a 'horizontal cordon' – it's a highly decorative tree form, making an unusual and productive edging to a path or bed and picking is made easy. The tree is trained on a single wire 18in (45cm) from the ground so that the tree forms a low barrier.

- Espalier: This consists of a central stem with horizontal arms set about 18in (45cm) apart. An espalier can be grown on free-standing posts and wires, or on a wall or fence. Although productive, these trees take longer to reach maturity than cordons.

PLANTS AND FLOWERS

BEGONIAS FROM SEED

Start begonias in mid-late winter to give them the long growing period they need.

By early spring there is a marked increase in daylight hours, and this is a sure sign it's time to sow seeds like begonias that need a long period to grow and flower.

There are two types of begonia you can grow from seed. One is the tender, annual fibrous-rooted bedding type, and the second is the tuberous begonia which develops a bulb-like tuber, and is a half-hardy perennial.

Begonia seeds need to be placed in a propagator or on a sunny windowsill in order to germinate. They are really tiny, and they need light for germination. For a high germination rate, the seed compost must be at room temperature, and sieved so the tiny seeds can lie on the top of it without being covered by large (in comparison) lumps.

A temperature of 20°C (68°F) is required until they are established, and the young plants need to be hardened off.

QUICK TIP

Begonia seed needs a sunny place to germination properly, but keep seedlings out of hot sun in spring.

It is best to scatter begonia seeds evenly over the compost surface. Therefore, it is best to use open seed trays or pots, not modular ones.

STEP BY STEP SOWING BEGONIA SEEDS

Fill a medium to small seed tray with sieved seed compost. Firm down and water; allow to drain, and let the compost to settle before sowing the seeds.

Mix unpelleted seeds with two teaspoons of sand in an old salt or flour shaker. Shake the mix evenly over the compost surface.

Then cover them with a plastic lid, or put in a clear plastic bag to stop the seeds drying out. Place on a sunny windowsill; keep the compost moist.

Pelleted begonia seeds

If you have difficulty handling begonia seeds, look out for pelleted ones, which are easier to handle and sow. These seeds are covered with a coating, which is soluble, dissolving when watered. The coating may also include nutrients and a fungicide to help protect the seedling.

NOTES:

A GOOD MONTH FOR THE ROSES

Bare-root, pre-packed and pot roses are all available in early spring, so get planting.

Roses are a versatile plant, easy to look after and will grow pretty much anywhere (barring the sandiest of soils) as long as they are placed in a sunny position, sheltered from strong winds, with plenty of room and food.

Choose the right site and you will be rewarded with healthy, strong growth and years of garden colour.

Avoid planting new roses where roses have been grown in the past. Doing so may cause the new plants to suffer from 'rose-sickness'. Symptoms include sluggish growth, and increased susceptibility to diseases.

You can use the same space for roses if you replace the soil to a depth of 18in (45cm) before planting.

Roses can be bought in three different ways, and all are best planted in mid-spring. Roses love soils rich in organic matter. Mixing in well-rotted manure a few weeks prior to planting will give them everything they need for good, early growth.

There is no need to add extra fertiliser to the planting hole providing plenty of organic matter has been added, but to maintain vigour, feed through the year.

So get to it, and plant a rose this spring.

QUICK TIP

When handling, planting or pruning traditional thorny-stemmed roses, always wear stout gloves!

KNOW YOUR ROSES

There is a rose out there to suit most garden situations. When choosing, assess the planting area and ask yourself what flower shape and colour you are after and the growth habit you require. Always research before buying a long lived plant.

IPC

• Bush roses
These roses have upright growth with large flowers. They usually have one flower per stem. Many varieties produce a second flush later in the year. Ideal in borders.

David Austin

• Standard roses
Many roses can be grown as a standard (long clear stem). Good for using to add height to borders, and can be underplanted. They do need some support – a tree post and tie is best.

WHICH TYPE OF ROSE TO BUY

Container roses

Container-grown roses can be bought and planted all year round to provide instant colour to borders, but they are the most expensive option. Planting them now gives the roses more time to establish in warm soils before autumn rain and frosts hit. Choose a specimen that is healthy, sturdy and has a good shape.

Bare-root roses

Bare-root roses are usually bought by mail order and dug out of the ground just before delivery. These plants have a large root spread. Cheaper than container roses, but can only be bought when roses are dormant. Plant as soon as possible. If the ground is frozen, heel-in until able to plant.

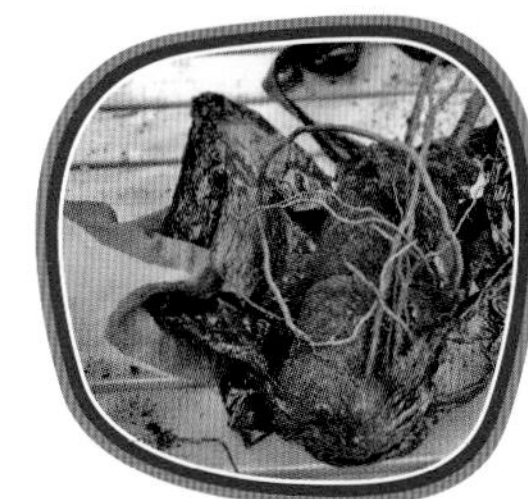

Pre-packed roses

Pre-packed roses are similar to bare-rooted; the only difference is that they are placed in a growing medium with their roots trimmed and wrapped tightly in either clear or black plastic. Usually the cheapest form to buy and available in many shops. Left on shop shelves too long they can start to sprout – only buy dormant plants.

HOW TO PLANT ROSES

- Prepare the site a few weeks prior to planting by digging in well-rotted manure, at least a bucketful to every square yard (square metre).
- Soak bare-root and wrapped roses in a bucket of water for a couple of hours before planting.
- Container roses need to be watered at least an hour before planting.
- If planting bare-rooted, dig a hole wide enough for the roots to be spread out.
- With container grown and pre-wrapped roses, tease out roots before planting.
- Plant the rose in the centre of the hole, making sure the graft is at soil level. This is seen as a bulge at the base.
- Backfill with soil and gently firm the rose in with the heel of your foot.
- On poor soils apply a general fertiliser around the base of the plant at 3oz per sq yd (80g per sq m) and lightly fork in, avoiding roots.

- If planting more than one rose, spacing will depend on the variety – check labels.
- For standard roses, hammer in a tree stake at an angle of 45 degrees. Attach using a tree tie.

David Austin

• Climber and rambler roses
Climbers and ramblers have strong upright growth, great for training on walls, fences and trellis. Rambling roses (not all) usually flower just once, while climbers tend to repeat flower.

IPC

• Patio roses
These roses were bred to combat the problem of many older style roses failing in container displays due to restricted root growth. These smaller plants are ideal for patios or balconies.

David Austin

• Modern shrub roses
Also known as the English rose, they are a cross between modern and old varieties. They usually have strong scent, with the repeat flowering habit of 'old roses'.

SPEEDY PERENNIALS

Sowing early will enable the plants to put on enough growth to flower later in the year and establish well in the ground before autumn.

Some perennials sown in the early months of the year will flower during summer, and year after year.

We are used to growing annuals for summer colour. They produce a splash of vibrant colour in summer. But after that the plants are finished and all we can do is compost them.

However with first-year flowering perennials, the story is very different. Just like annuals we sow them in early spring for flowering in summer. But then the plants will perform just as all perennials do, by surviving over the winter and repeating their displays for many years to come.

Lots of perennials take a couple of years to flower from seed but now, thanks to plant breeders, there is a large group of hardy perennials that will flower in their first year after sowing, although they may bloom slightly later in the year.

To give these perennials the best chance of flowering in their first year, it is essential to start them off early. Late winter to early spring is a good time; light levels are increasing and after germination they will rapidly put on growth if exposed to the right conditions. And if you are keen to grow lots of perennials, sowing these first-year varieties will save you money (sowing a packet of seeds is a lot cheaper than buying mature plants!).

It is fair to say that it is not always 100 per cent guaranteed that you will have flowers in the first summer after sowing, as certain variables (such as weather, soil and plant hormones) may put a block on flower production. However, the chance of colour is generally very good with specific cultivars and, unlike annuals, you will always be sure that flowers will be had in the second year, and thereafter.

QUICK TIP

Give plants the best chance of success by mulching annually in spring or autumn with 2-3in (5-7.5cm) of rotted manure.

DAMPING OFF

This is a soil-borne fungal disease that can affect all seedlings. Symptoms include i) failure of seedling to emerge, and ii) emerged seedlings suddenly collapse or die back. It is more common in seedlings raised under glass, and at this time of year when light levels and temperatures are still not at their peak. To reduce the chance of damping off, follow these tips:

- Sow seedlings in fresh, sterile compost.
- Use clean pots and trays.
- Sow seeds thinly to avoid overcrowding.
- Water with tap water (rather than rainwater).
- Ensure adequate ventilation around young plants.

If you've had damping off problems in the past, use a fruit and vegetable disease control as a preventative measure (but following all the above advice should reduce the need for using it).

AFTERCARE

- Keep plants under cover until all risk of frost has passed. Pot on as necessary.
- Harden off the young plants gradually (bring them outside during the day, and in again at night).
- Don't allow the plants whilst growing in pots to dry out, but do not over-water either.
- Prepare the planting site in advance; remove weeds and break up the soil with a garden fork to at least the depth of the garden fork.
- Prior to planting, dig in organic matter such as well-rotted manure or compost.
- After planting your perennials, scatter a balanced slow-release fertiliser on the soil.
- Remove weeds when small so they do not grow through the plants.
- Do not divide new perennials until they are at least three years old.

TREES TO PLANT IN POTS

Set trees during late winter while bare root plants are still available.

Buying bare root trees is a great way to start a collection of patio trees on a budget, and late winter is the time to do it.

Don't ever think your garden is too small for trees. Even patio and balcony gardeners can enjoy small trees by growing them in large containers.

Whether you want to make a move into small-scale fruit production, or just want to add a new element of height, structure and seasonal interest, there is a tree out there to suit.

QUICK TIP

Make sure grafting points remain above the compost surface when potting up.

DO IT NOW

5 simple steps to planting a tree in a large container

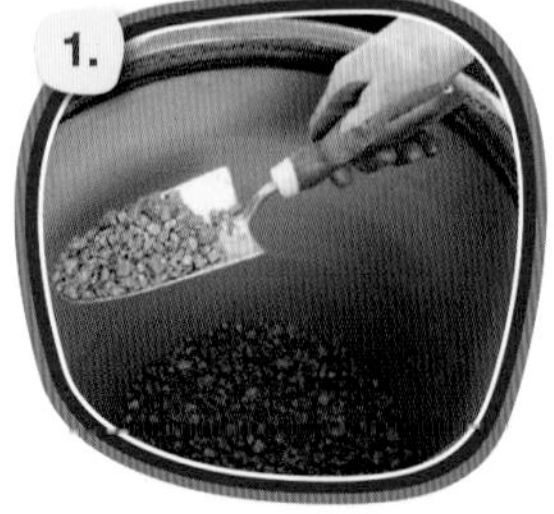

1. Line the bottom of a heavy, frost-proof pot (min. 18in/45cm diameter) with a 2in (5cm) layer of gravel or broken pot pieces to aid drainage.

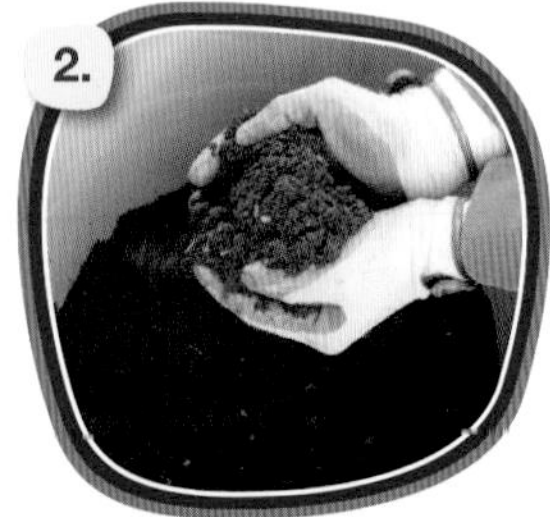

2. Part fill with compost, firming in by poking your fingers down into the compost. Check levels by sitting the roots of the tree in the pot.

CHOOSING YOUR TREES

Fruit trees in containers won't produce yields like you'd get from a 'field grown' tree. With this in mind, it makes sense to go for something a little different.

There are a few rules to follow when setting trees in pots. Firstly, choose the best pot you can afford. Go for a terracotta or clay pot (or wooden for an apple tree), glazed to protect it against frost, and heavy enough to weigh down your tree in strong winds.

You don't want to be potting on your trees every year either, so go for a big pot at least 18in (45cm) across. Using the right compost will also help.

Lots of trees grafted onto dwarfing rootstocks are suited to pot growing. Some large types like eucalyptus and willow also work, if coppiced in winter.

If you've a tree in mind, ask the retailer before buying, whether it will cope in a pot.

Trees for fruit

Quince comes on a dwarf rootstock to offer an eventual height and spread of around 3ft (1m) with formative pruning It is self-fertile and does not require a pollination companion. It should produce fruit after about three years. Cherry 'Griotella' is a naturally dwarf tree, having being grafted onto a dwarf rootstock. (It will reach a mature height of around 5ft (1.5m)). No pollination companion is needed to get its sharp tasting fruits, which will be great for cooking.

T&M

Trees for flower and foliage

Popular container trees include acers, conifers, apples, pears, plums, peaches, nectarines and topiary such as yew and box. Potting tender trees such as olives and citrus allows you to bring them undercover for winter protection.

8treetyme.co.uk

3. Once the soil mark at the base of the main stem is sitting an inch or so below the pot rim, set the tree centrally and fan out the roots as best you can.

4. Fill up the pot with more compost, shaking the stem up and down to work the compost in between the roots. Finally, firm in really well.

5. Pot compost dries quickly in winter wind and summer sun, so apply a moisture-retaining stone mulch on the surface. Water in and stake if necessary.

SOWING HARDY ANNUAL SEEDS

Gypsophila paniculata can be difficult to grow direct in garden soil. Starting it off in pots, then planting it out, solves the problem.

Hardy annuals can be sown under cover with no extra warmth.

Hardy annuals are easy to grow – they provide cheap seasonal colour in the summer months, and are perfect for many areas of the garden. They are the type of annual that, once germinated, can even withstand a light frost.

You can sow hardy annuals in late winter with bottom heat, but they require a deal of care and attention. However, once the days are longer and temperatures are rising, they can be sown with just a little protection from the elements, such as a cold frame or unheated greenhouse. They don't need extra warmth in order to germinate.

It is still slightly too early to directly sow hardy annuals into garden soil, as late frosts could still discourage the seeds from starting into growth.

Making an early sowing now allows you to transplant the youngsters into their final positions once they are sturdy little plants, so helping them to survive against slugs, snails and birds that will all happily chomp and obliterate seedlings.

Some hardy annuals, however, do not like to be transplanted and are best sown direct. For these annuals use coir pots or seed plugs so they can be planted out in their pots, with little root disturbance.

QUICK TIP

If you do not have a cold frame or greenhouse, place the sown seeds under a cloche for protection.

HARDY ANNUALS FOR DIFFERENT AREAS

For cut flowers

Many annuals can be grown successfully for cut flowers. Try any of these to decorate your home throughout the summer months:

- *Gypsophila paniculata*
- *Orlaya grandiflora*
- *Ammi majus (bishop's flower)*
- *Linaria maroccana 'Sweeties'*
- *Malope trifida 'Vulcan'*
- *Bupleurum rotundifolium*
- *Chrysanthemum carinatum*

For containers

Pots and containers will brighten up any garden; the following annuals are all suitable for growing in restricted places, such as baskets, pots and window boxes:

- *Lathyrus odoratus 'Pink Cupid'*
- *Calendula officinalis nana 'Fruit Twist'*
- *Viola x wittrockiana (pansy)*
- *Sanvitalia procumbens*

For attracting wildlife

Growing flowers native to our country not only looks great, but they are less hard work to look after! Sow the following to help insects and other wildlife:

- *Helianthus annuus (sunflower)*
- *Limnanthes douglasii (poached egg plant)*
- *Centaurea cyanus (cornflower)*
- *Echium vulgare 'Blue Bedder'*

SOIL PREP FOR OUTDOOR SOWING

Prepare border soil now for sowing hardy annuals outdoors in spring. Dig the soil to the depth of a spade's blade, and remove all weeds. Add organic matter such as well-rotted garden compost. Leave to settle for 2-3 weeks then sow.

For easy self-seeding

Some hardy annuals are great for self seeding, which means you get 'free' plants year-after-year. Sow the following to reap the benefits of this:

- *Cerinthe major*
- *Borago officinalis (borage)*
- *Consolida ajacis (larkspur)*
- *Lobularia (formerly alyssum)*

For attractive seedheads

Many hardy annuals produce seedheads that will give you the added bonus of winter interest. They can also be dried and used indoors. Try growing the following:

- *Papaver somniferum*
- *Nigella damascena (love-in-a-mist)*
- *Lunaria annua (honesty)*
- *Agrostemma githago (corn cockle)*

SOWING SUNFLOWERS

Start off a crop of cheery sunflowers – here's the long and short of what to do!

We all love a sunflower.And you, too, can fill your garden with those cheery blooms in summer. Sow the seeds before the end of April for beds and borders of colour. Of course there is always the competition you can have with yourself (or others) to see how tall your plants will eventually become.

Plant breeders have created dozens of sunflower varieties, so it's worth searching for the ones that best suit your requirements.

HOW TO GROW

Sow your sunflower seeds into large, multi-celled modular trays. Mix a sowing compost comprising an equal ratio of loam, perlite and sand. Label and water the trays, then stand them in a warm propagator in the greenhouse. Germination will take seven to ten days.

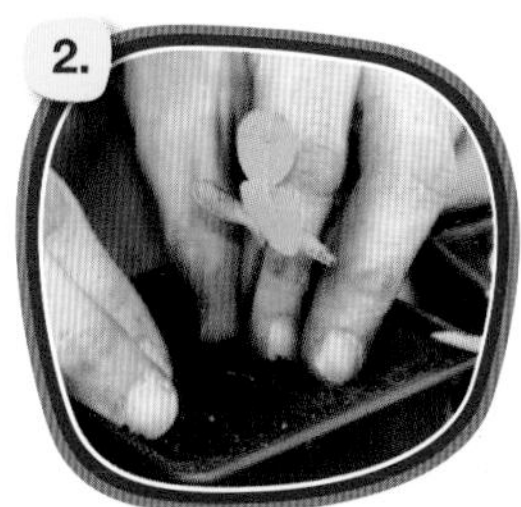

When the seedlings are an inch or two high, pot them up individually into 3½in (9cm) pots. Harden them off before planting outside.

Plant out early summer. Choose a sunny spot. Plant large varieties 15in (38cm) apart, dwarf ones 9-10in (23-25cm) apart.

Not all sunflowers are monsters that grow as tall as a house:

'Aslan'

is a quick-growing dwarf sunflower bearing bright flowers of a rich lemon yellow. Ideal for cutting. To 3ft (90cm).

'Vanilla Ice'

produces masses of pale yellow flowers, each with a contrasting chocolate-coloured centre. To 5ft (1.5m).

'Infrared F1'

is an amazing range of bicolour shades on multi-stemmed plants. Bees love the nectar. To 6ft (1.8m).

'Helianthus maximilliani'

is a perennial sunflower. Its golden yellow blooms have a fragrance like chocolate. To 6ft 6in (2m).

RHODODENDRONS FOR QUICK COLOUR

Bring some much needed colour to the garden with early season rhododendrons.

We are all in need of a colour fix after the drab of winter.

You don't need acidic soil to grow these rhododendrons – they perform great in containers and there are even varieties that are lime tolerant for use in low pH or neutral soils.

Half a whisky barrel makes an unusual and visually stunning container to plant your rhododendrons – why not give it a try?

QUICK TIP

Stand pots to soak in a bucket of water for 20 minutes before planting.

STEP BY STEP

Rustic Rhodo barrel

1. If your local garden centre doesn't have the real thing, it should offer a half barrel 'style' container. If you manage to get a real whisky barrel, you'll need to drill drainage holes.

2. Cover the drainage holes with rocks then add a layer of grit or gravel to improve drainage. This will also help weigh down the container – rhododendrons can get to good sizes and be top heavy in pots.

PLANTING IN THE GROUND

It is hard to permanently adjust alkaline (chalky) soil with the addition of ericaceous compost – over time it will revert. If you already have acidic soils then the widest range of rhododenrons are at your disposal. If you have neutral or alkaline soil your best option is to choose one of the new lime tolerant varieties. Around 40 varieties are now available.

Rhododendrons stand up to sun or shade, but semi-shade is best. They need an 'open soil', so add plenty of leaf mould or compost to heavy clay soils before planting.

Set the plant in a hole not much deeper than the rootball, but wide enough to add a mix of soil and compost back around the rootball. Firm in well, setting the rootball just below the surface. Water in. If planting an acid loving variety, try to only ever use stored rain water.

FEEDING

Pot compost should provide enough feed for a good few months – running out in summer just as plants are starting to develop their flower buds for next year. Through summer start to apply a fortnightly liquid feed. For best results opt for a specialist feed.

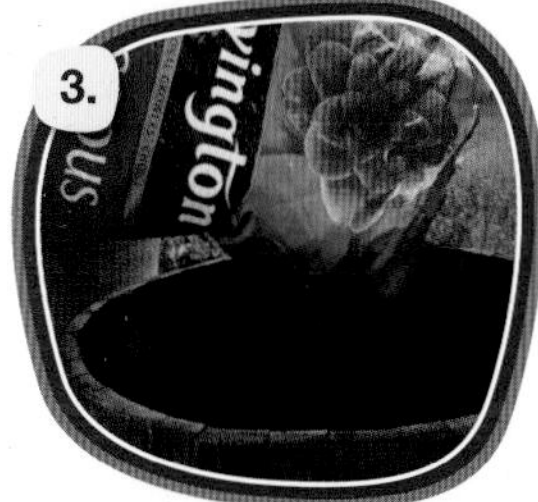

Part fill with ericaceous compost, checking the level by placing the plant in the pot. Rhododendrons like moist soil, so aim to leave a good few inches of container rim exposed so the plant can be heavily watered in summer.

Set the plant centrally in the pot, teasing out dense roots by scratching over the surface. Pack around the rootball with more ericaceous compost, firming in as you go until level with the top of the rootball.

Water in to settle the compost. This may sink as the water drains so be prepared to top up levels. Sit back and within a few weeks all those buds should have burst into colour to finally help get the season off to a start.

WONDERFUL WISTERIA

Wisterias are climbers with scented purple, pink or white flowers, that are ideal for planting against a wall.

They can also be trained to scramble over pergolas, fencing and other garden structures.

They prefer to grow in a sunny position, but can tolerate slight shade. The best soil for them is well-drained fertile soil, but if you have poor, sandy soil they will grow but will need to be watered regularly so they do not dry out. Feed wisteria in spring with fish, blood and bone, to encourage the formation of flowering buds. On poor soils apply sulphate of potash at the rate of 1oz per sq yd (35g per m3).

Wisterias are easier to care for than you think. Planted and pruned correctly, you will be rewarded with beautiful flowers for years to come.

BUYING WISTERIA

It is best to buy a wisteria plant in flower as this indicates it is a mature specimen; otherwise you may have to wait a couple of years for the blooms. Nurseries propagate wisterias by grafting or by taking cuttings and these produce flowering plants quicker than if raised from seed (which takes many years).

Grafted specimens have a visible bulge near the base of the main stem.

If space is short, *Wisteria frutescens* 'Amethyst Falls' is a slightly more compact cultivar that can grow in pots or be trained up smaller structures.

PRUNING WISTERIA

These climbers need to be pruned twice a year to keep them flowering and growing within their allotted space.

In summer, pruning is done to control its size and shape and to encourage the plant to form flower buds for next year's show.

In winter, pruning involves tidying up the main framework before it blooms.

DID YOU KNOW?

There are two common types of wisteria available from garden centres: *Wisteria sinensis*, which flowers before the foliage, and *Wisteria floribunda* which produces buds and foliage at the same time.

HOW TO PLANT WISTERIA

- Water the wisteria well in its pot and allow to drain.
- Fix strong training wires to the wall you plan to grow it up, before planting.
- Dig a generous hole 18in (45cm) out from the wall.
- Add a few handfuls of well rotted organic matter to the base of the hole and fork in.
- If the soil is poor, add a general fertiliser, such as growmore, into the hole.
- Remove the plant from its pot and tease out some of the roots from the compost.
- Place the wisteria in the planting hole, ensuring that it is set at the same level as it was in the pot.
- If planting against a wall or trellis, angle the plant slightly towards the frame.
- Fill around the rootball with soil and gently firm the plant in its new home.
- Water in well.

NOTES:

PLANTING DAHLIAS

Fill your garden with the glorious different flower shapes of the dahlia.

Dahlias are perennial plants that grow from tubers or seed. There are thousands of varieties available in different sizes, colour and flower shapes.

The best time to plan t tubers is in early summer, after the risk of frost has passed. You can also buy young dahlia plants in pots from garden centres.

You may see dahlias sold as bedding plants. These cultivars have been grown from seed and do not grow very tall. They will form tubers over the year, and they can be saved for the year after, but for that big hit of colour in your border, choose those grown from tubers in two litre pots from garden centres.

Dahlias grow best in a sunny position in a fertile, moist soil with good drainage. A few days before planting, mix in some well-rotted organic matter to give them a good start. With regular feeding and watering they will produce a spectacular display in any size garden, flowering late into autumn.

To stop the stems breaking on dahlia plants, they will require staking at planting time. Tie in new growth every couple of weeks.

STEP BY STEP

Dig out a 6in (15cm) hole for tubers. For young plants dig a hole slightly wider and deeper than the pot. Add a sprinkling of general fertiliser.

Place the tubers in the hole. If planting containerised dahlias, water, allow to drain, then plant at the same depth it was in the pot.

Place stakes around the tubers or plant before you backfill with soil. This ensures the stakes are in position without damaging the tubers.

USING IN BORDERS

Dahlias look stunning in mixed borders. Do allow enough space around them to grow as they can become rather large. Plant in rows 30in (75cm) apart, near the front of borders so they are easily accessible if you want to cut a few flowers for indoors.

USING IN CONTAINERS

There are many smaller varieties of dahlia that look great in mixed containers . These can be planted from tubers, or in growth. Choose a container at least 12in (30cm) wide and deep. Plant tubers around 6in (15cm) deep. Set plants at same depth as in pot. Use multipurpose compost and mix in a slow release feed. Don't let the compost dry out.

FEEDING AND WATERING

Dahlias are hungry plants and even after correct planting in fertile soil they will need a liquid feed high in potassium every two weeks, once flower buds appear. Feeding them on a regular basis will encourage the plant to produce more flower buds. Water regularly, especially in summer, giving a good soaking of water every couple of days.

BEAUTIFUL BIENNIALS

Sow seeds for a stunning display of colourful flowers next year.

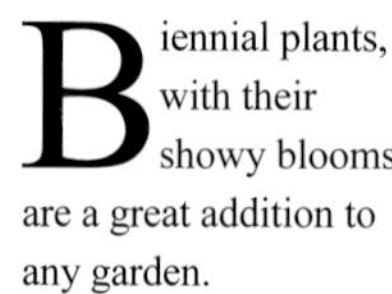

Biennials look stunning in mixed borders, and many, like sweet smelling stocks are great to use in cut flower displays.

Biennial plants, with their showy blooms are a great addition to any garden.

They are a group of plants that overwinter to complete their life cycle.

In the first year they germinate, grow roots and form a clump of leaves. Then over the colder months they die back and go dormant. The next year, the plants burst back into life, producing flowers and setting seed before they die.

Many biennials self seed easily, so the lifecycle starts again. You'll hardly notice, as the new plants grow near to the old parent plant.

You can scatter seeds of biennials, on bare patches of soil between other plants, covering lightly with soil.

If you would rather sow in a controlled manner, there are numerous ways to do so (below). You don't even need to buy special compost, as a multipurpose is fine to use.

QUICK TIP

If sowing direct in borders, label the area. This will stop young growth being mistaken for weeds.

3 WAYS TO SOW

• Seed beds
To sow lots of different biennials, create a seedbed in a unused patch of soil. Dig over to remove weeds and large stones. Rake level to create a fine surface, and then sow the seeds in drills and label. Once germinated, prick out into individual pots, or transplant in autumn.

• Trays or pots
In exposed gardens and those with a slug problem, sow biennials in trays or pots to keep in a coldframe for protection. When large enough, prick out seedlings and pot them up individually. Pot on again so they can produce a large root system, before planting out.

• A different approach
If you are tight on space, sow seeds in guttering, about 3-5ft (1 -1.5m) in length. Fill with moist compost and sow in a zigzag pattern. Once seedlings appear, thin out. A few weeks later, make a trench the same size as the guttering and slide plants into the trench.

SIX OF THE BEST BIENNIALS TO TRY

J Swithinbank

Wikimedia SB_Johnny

Dianthus barbatus (Sweet Williams)
Many dianthus are actually perennials, but are grown as biennials. Grow in well-drained soil, which is neutral to slightly acid, in full sun.

Hesperis matronalis (Sweet rocket)
Sweet rocket will grow in shade or full sun, flowering in early summer. The soil should be well-drained, light and on the dry side.

Verbascum bombyciferum (Mullein)
With stunning foliage these plants look great used as dot plants. They are drought-tolerant, preferring a light and sandy well-drained soil.

Suttons

Erysimum cheiri (Wallflower)
Sowing these from seed will give you a wider choice of cultivars than buying bare root plants in autumn from garden centres. Grow in well-drained soil in full sun.

Matthiola incana (Stocks)
Heavily scented, they are great to use as a cut flower for indoor displays. Stocks happily grow in moist, fertile soils that are not acidic. Plant and grow them in a sheltered site with full sun.

Digitalis purpurea (Foxglove)
A native flower, the biennial foxglove will grow in almost any soil except very dry or wet locations. You can sow or plant in sun, part or full shade, in exposed or sheltered sites.

BIENNIALS IN BORDERS

Sowing biennials from seed is a cost effective way to create drifts of colour in borders. Use them in groups, through a border, or use taller varieties as dot plants between perennials. They also work well used as spring bedding, as many will flower early from a late winter sowing.

LILIES IN POTS

Here's how to plant lily bulbs into pots and containers for flowering next summer.

1. Place a 2in (5cm) layer of drainage material, such as crocks or small stones, in the base of your chosen container, before beginning to fill it with potting compost.

2. A 9in (23cm) wide container will take one large lily bulb – 4-5in (10-12cm) in diameter – or three to four smaller bulbs 2-3in (5-8cm) in diameter. For more bulbs use a bigger container – and they should always be 12in (30cm) or more deep. Allow 2in (5cm) between bulbs.

3. Plant Asiatic hybrid lilies (which produce roots from the base of the bulb) and those whose rooting habit is unknown, at a depth equal to the height of the bulb. Plant stem-rooting lilies at a depth roughly two-and-a-half times the height of the bulb. The pointed tip of the bulb scales should always be pointing upwards.

4. Any good multipurpose compost is suitable. Pot lime-hating lilies into ericaceous compost.

5. Lilies are heavy feeders, so add granules of a controlled-release fertiliser when planting.

6. Many lilies will be fully hardy and can be left outside in larger containers all year round. It may be a good idea, however, to wrap the containers over winter with a sheet of bubble polythene to keep out the worst of the frost. In very cold areas, keep containers in frost-free greenhouses or sheds until spring.

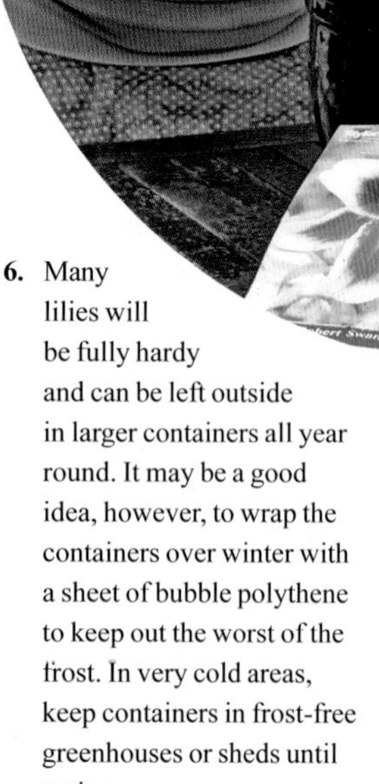

Deep containers are best for lilies, especially the larger bulbs such as the Asiatic hybrid Lilium 'Lollypop'.

Lilies usually need cool winter conditions if they are to flower well the following summer, so bringing them into the house over winter is not a good idea.

HONEY FUNGUS

This is the most destructive fungal disease in gardens, according to many experts. It is actually the single name given to several different species of fungi that attack and kill the roots of many woody and perennial plants.

Signs of attack are honey coloured toadstools appearing on infected stumps. Peel off a bit of bark at ground level and you'll see white fungal growth between the bark and wood.

Upper parts of the plant die, and leaves are often smaller, and paler-than-average. There is often either no flowering, or an unusually heavy flowering followed by a heavy crop of fruit (just before the plant dies).

There are no chemicals to control it. Dig up and destroy (by burning) all infected stumps and roots. To prevent spread, lay a physical barrier – such as an 18in (45cm) deep vertical strip of butyl rubber (pond liner) buried in the soil. Allow it to protrude slightly above soil level.

All plants are vulnerable, but some (including yew, heather, bamboo, berberis, box and blueberry) have good resistance.

These plants are thought to be most susceptible to honey fungus:

- Acer (except *Acer negundo*)
- Horse chestnut
- Birch *(Betula)*
- Butterfly bush *(Buddleja)*
- Californian alilac *(Ceanothus)*
- Cedar
- Leyland cypress
- Beech *(Fagus)*
- Hydrangea
- Holly *(Ilex)*
- Privet *(Ligustrum)*
- Magnolia
- Apple *(Malus)*
- Pear *(Pyrus)*
- Rhododendron
- Currants *(Ribes)*
- Roses
- Willow *(Salix)*
- Lilac *(Syringa)*
- Viburnum

PLANTING CLIMBERS

Setting out perennial climbers and wall shrubs.

Climbers and wall shrubs are a crucial part of the planting palette in any garden, but they become most important in small gardens where there is little space for planting. In such places, walls and fences should be utilised in order to pack in as much foliage and flower as possible.

The space in the lee of a fence or wall is termed a 'rain shadow'. Rain rarely falls straight down, and a fence or wall will prevent angled rain from falling on the soil on the sheltered side. The most important thing to remember when planting climbers is to set them at least 12in (30cm) away from the wall/ fence and angle them backwards to their supports so their roots avoid the rain shadow as much as possible.

All climbers – even self-clinging types – will need some help to establish themselves, and a support of some form is needed. The most common options are trelliswork, horizontal wires and obelisks, and these need to be in place before planting your chosen climber.

QUICK TIP

Metal spirals can be used to support lightweight climbers in pots or confined spaces, and they give a modern feel.

STEP BY STEP

How to plant a climber:

Dig a planting hole 12-18in (30-45cm) out from the wall/ fence and set the climber at an angle, pointing canes and stems towards the support.

Cut away the plastic ties, and untwine the stems – but keep the canes in place in order to train the plant towards the trellis or wires.

Tendrils and twiners

Many popular climbers simply twine (or spiral) their stems around their supports. Others have searching tendrils at regular intervals along their stems, which seek out support and wrap around it to take hold. Honeysuckle is a prime example of a twining climber, and Virginia Creeper is a tendril climber. Twiners and those with tendrils are best trained to trelliswork. Once established, your only job will be to check for wayward growths and tuck them back to the trellis to keep things tidy.

Wall shrubs

Wall shrubs are so-named because they are best placed under the shelter and/or warmth of a wall – but they have no natural ability to cling or twine. To keep them against their support they will need regular tying-in as the growing season progresses. They will also need occasional pruning to get them to grow in the direction you want them.

Horizontal wires are the best type of support for wall shrubs.

Self clingers

Some climbers will attach themselves to walls and fences using grasping aerial roots along their stems. Ivy is a prime example. However, for a more decorative option plant *Hydrangea petiolaris*. Training wires are needed to hold it in place until later growth attaches to the wall. It might be necessary to prune out some inward-pointing growths that prevent you from setting it close to the wall. Softer, outward-facing growth could be pulled back to the wires, but stiffer stems must be cut away.

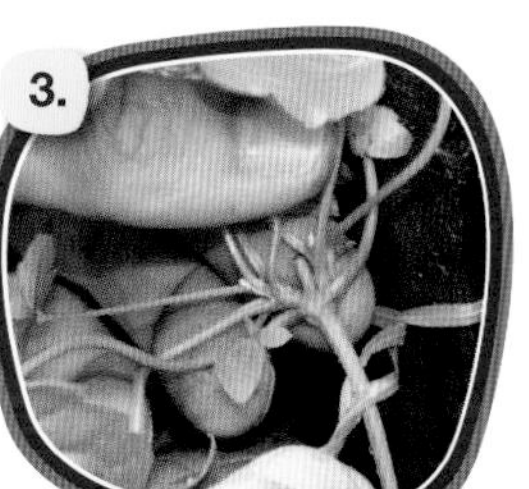

3.

Untangle the stems and fan them out for good coverage of the support. Re-tie them to the canes, attaching the tips to the supports.

4.

Having secured the best stems, remove weak, twiggy and misplaced growths. Cut away outward growing stems of wall shrubs.

5.

Give the plant a heavy watering to settle soil around the rootball, then apply a mulch to help retain moisture and suppress weeds.

SEASONS

BASKET MAKEOVER

Refresh winter pots and baskets ready for spring.

Adding spring blooms will inject colour back into the garden.

Your seasonal hanging baskets and containers will have succumbed to the winter weather.

New bedding plants and spring bulbs can be picked up cheaply, so there's little point in keeping plants that have been affected by pests and diseases, at the risk of spreading problems to other plants.

Late winter and early spring can still take their toll on young flowers; buy varieties that will tolerate late frosts and have some fleece to hand, to protect them if needed.

Winter rain will likely have flushed out the nutrients from container composts, so remove the top 2in (5cm) and replace with fresh compost, and start feeding fortnightly.

QUICK TIP

When renovating pots and baskets, buy plants that have been grown outdoors or hardened off before sale.

STEP BY STEP Bringing colour to your winter displays

1. Decide which plants can stay in your displays and tie these back with an old hair band or string to give you better access to the plants around them.

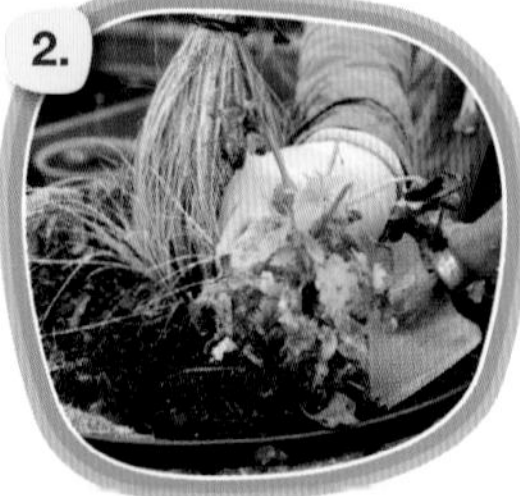

2. Remove all old, diseased and dead plants that you want to replace, taking care not to damage or cut into the roots of the plants you want to keep.

3. Scrape away as much compost as possible, without disturbing or damaging remaining plants. Use your hands or a small trowel to do this.

CONTAINER CONTROL

Raised off the ground and hung from chains, hanging baskets are pretty safe from the ravages of hungry slugs and snails, but patio containers are prime targets. Not only are they a convenient meal for these slimy scoundrels, pot rims and the space created by pot feet are perfect hiding places, allowing them to remain undetected by day before coming out under cover of darkness to do their damage.

As you re-dress your containers lift them up and check for hiding molluscs and dispose of as you see fit. At this time of year it is too cold to apply nematode mixes as a biological control. If you can't deal with picking molluscs off by hand, slug pellets scattered on compost and under pots, or barriers such as copper tape, grit and eggshells are the best option until late spring. Check over new additions before planting.

REPLACEMENT PLANTS

Bedding:

- Primula
- Pansy
- Viola
- Cyclamen
- Hyacinth

Bulbs:

- Narcissus
- Anemone
- Snakes Head Fritillary
- Iris reticulata
- Crocus
- Snowdrops
- Tulips
- Hyacinth

Foliage:

- Ornamental cabbage
- Evergreens
- Grasses
- Ivy
- Ferns

Feeding for flowering success

You can usually forego feeding containers through winter, but if it has been very wet, rainfall will likely have washed much of the nutrient content out of compost in winter, leaving little to keep plants thriving through to summer.

With spring bulbs and bedding plants coming back into active growth, they will need a boost to keep them at their best, particularly if the bulbs are to be used again next year – they need to be able to take on stored nutrients for good repeat performance.

As you tidy your displays feed the plants with an all purpose feed, containing the major nutrients required for healthy flower, foliage and root development. This can be done two ways. Either apply a slow release fertiliser at replanting time, or adopt a liquid feed regime, applying at fortnightly intervals until flowering stops, and in the case of bulbs, when the leaves, have all died down.

4. To save money and spread new colour across the display, separate plants and bulbs in pots. Prise apart gently, making sure each plant has good roots.

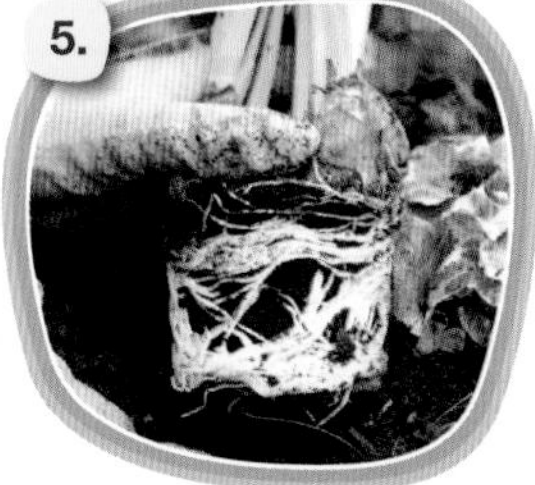

5. Set the new plants, adding fresh multipurpose compost to fill spaces. Really pack the pot/basket full with plants for extra impact.

6. Untie existing plants and tidy by removing dead leaves and flowers. Ornamental grasses can be trimmed or combed through to remove dead foliage.

EARLY SPRING CUTTINGS

Some of your garden plants will offer early material for propagation.

In mid-spring there is a very specific form of cuttings propagation that cannot be undertaken at any other time of year.

Whereas semi-ripe cuttings are taken in summer, hardwood cuttings in autumn and root cuttings in winter – now is the time to take stem-tip cuttings from the soft, short-jointed young shoots of the many plants that are just beginning to sprout after the winter rest.

A word of caution: be gentle with all these early cuttings as they lose water and wilt quickly. They are also vulnerable to bruising, which may expose the foliage and stems to attack from fungal rots.

FUCHSIAS

Both hardy border fuchsias and the tender bedding, greenhouse or conservatory 'pot' fuchsias will be shooting from the base now. With a sharp knife or razor blade, carefully slice off the shoot – ideally 1½-2½in (3-6cm) long. Cut under a leaf joint and pinch out the growing tip. Dip the base in rooting hormone, and insert in a moist cuttings compost in a pot. Keep on a windowsill indoors with filtered sunlight, or in a greenhouse. Mist the leaves daily.

HEATHERS

All of the textbooks say to take semi-ripe cuttings of heathers (calluna and erica) in the summer. But it is certainly worth taking some softwood tip cuttings now. Select shoots that are healthy, vigorous and non-flowering.

Each cutting should be 1½-3in (3-7.5cm) long. With finger and thumb, strip the leaves from the bottom half of the cutting, and pinch out the very tip with your nails. Pot up as for the fuchsias.

BIRDS IN SPRING

Even though winter is over, wild birds still need our help.

Feed birds in spring – they need to build themselves up after winter, and they need plenty of the right kinds of food when rearing young.

Although garden birds benefit most from us providing food for them during winter, natural food shortages can occur at any time of the year.

The breeding season, particularly, is a time when birds should not go hungry, so feeding now can make a huge difference to the survival of the nestlings.

Birds time their breeding periods to exploit the availability of natural food; members of the tit and chaffinch family go for caterpillars, whilst blackbirds and song thrushes go for earthworms.

It is now known that if the weather turns cold or wet during spring, severe shortages of insect food can occur, whilst in exceptionally dry weather, earthworms will be unavailable because of hard soil.

QUICK TIP

Don't put out tinned dog or cat food for birds. Some will eat it, but you may also attract magpies, crows and rats.

So, what should you put out during the spring months? From the kitchen you can put out mild grated cheese, soaked sultanas, raisins, currants, grapes, small pieces of soft apples, pears and bananas.

Bought products for wild birds in spring include black sunflower seeds, pinhead oatmeal, bird seed 'food bars', mealworms, waxworms, mixes for insectivorous birds, and general spring seed mixtures (without loose peanuts).

Garden centre shelves are filled with all of these products and more, but just now it is worth looking out for those aimed specifically at nesting and young birds.

There are things to avoid, too. Don't use peanuts, bread and fat in spring, as these can be bad if adult birds feed them to their young. If you have to supply peanuts, only do so in mesh feeders that won't allow large pieces to be given to the young and risk choking them.

Home-made fatballs can go soft and rancid in hot weather, so should not be supplied in late spring and summer.

You can also take softwood cuttings of the following now:

- Ampelopsis
- Aubrieta deltoides
- Rhododendron/azalea (deciduous forms only)
- Butterfly bush (buddleja)
- Caryopteris
- Corylopsis
- Fremontia
- Hebe 'Eveline'
- Lemon verbena (lippia)
- Magnolia
- Maple (acer)
- Mock orange (philadelphus)
- Virginia creeper parthenocissus)

Wikicommons/Endogen

Graham Clarke

SEASONAL CATCHUP

Catch up with those spring jobs before summer.

It is important to catch up on gardening tasks now. If certain tasks are left it is very easy for the garden to just end up looking a mess. In the warmer months, watering, summer pruning, pest control, harvesting and training take up our time. Prune shrubs that flower after mid-summer now to encourage new blooms on this year's growth. Sort out the shed, and most important of all, check the barbecue is clean and working - you never know!

1.

Tidy up the garden

Remove any seed heads and old plant stems left on perennials. This will allow new growth on them to develop freely.

Hoe between plants to remove weeds. Then check the plants over, pruning out any dead stems and other material damaged by the harsh start to spring. Clear away leaves and other debris from lawns to avoid the risk of fungal infections.

Dig over soil

Single dig bare patches of borders to improve the soil structure and drainage. Single digging means, turning over the soil to a garden fork or spade's depth.

Standing on a wooden board, dig a trench a spades depth deep and put the soil to one side, add well rotted organic matter to the trench.

Dig another trench alongside and place removed soil into the first trench on top of the organic matter.

Repeat as needed, filling the last.

2.

3.

Transplant

If you have not been able to move deciduous shrubs to a new location, there is still time if the plant is less than five years old and still dormant.

Evergreens can also be moved, as they need warm soil for root establishment.

Prepare the new site in advance. On poor soils add well rotted organic matter to the soil being used to back fill.

Ensure the hole is wide enough for roots to spread out. Keep well watered and do not let the roots dry out in the first few days.

4.

Sow and pot on

Annuals, biennials and perennials can all be sown now. They will germinate quickly as the soil is warmer, rapidly catching up with early sown varieties. Annual flowers sown now will give a late flourish of colour in early autumn, extending the season. Pot on bedding plants, seedlings and cuttings that have taken so they are in fresh compost and a suitable size pot for further growth and establishment, ready to plant out in their final positions later in the year.

5. Install automatic watering systems

Be prepared for hot dry spells, by setting up irrigation systems from water butts. Fit water timers onto outdoor taps connected to drip hoses, to help water borders and pots. Set up irrigation systems for growbags. Place seeping hoses in borders now before plant growth makes it difficult. Check garden hoses and any spray and sprinkler attachments for damage and replace if required.

6.

Check tree ties and climber supports

Check that tree support posts are secure in the ground and that ties are not too tight, or cutting into the bark. Ensure wall wires are taut and new growth is tied in, so it does not move about. This will decrease the chance of stems chafing.

7.

Mulch to retain water and reduce weeds

Make the most out of the wet start to spring, by mulching around plants with bark chippings or well-rotted organic matter to trap moisture.

8.

Repair structures

Repair fences and other structures before plant growth blocks access to them. Clean all garden furniture, and if wood, treat with a wood preserver. Coat wooden raised beds with boiled linseed oil to increase their longevity.

Tidy as you go

Clean used pots and trays before storing away over summer. If left dirty when stacked, the soil and any plant material in them could harbour pests and diseases.Keep garden tools sharp and clean ready for use.

9.

10.

Houseplants

Summer is a period of rapid growth for many indoor plants. Some timely care now will ensure healthy plants: Wipe leaves with a damp cloth, removing dust so they make the most of light levels.

Move houseplants to a cool, light place as temperatures rise to avoid wilting. Choose a slow release fertiliser for houseplants; spike drip feeders are available for foliage and flowering plants. Re-pot if required into fresh houseplant compost using a pot one size bigger.

HOW TO PLANT SUMMER BULBS

Get summer-flowering bulbs in now for hot colour in borders and pots.

Many summer bulbs, corms or tubers can be planted in early spring to create stunning displays in the garden.

The best time to plant summer-flowering bulbs, is from early spring until early summer. Frost tender bulbs are best planted last, after the risk of frost has passed. They can be started off in containers in the greenhouse and planted out later. Bulbs like to grow in free-draining soil with some well-rotted organic matter dug into it. If you are planting in heavy clay soil, mix in two buckets of coarse sand to every square metre of soil.

At this stage in spring, plant the bulbs quickly; leaving them in bags for too long will result in poor flowering.

Freesias can be planted in pots or in the ground, but only after the last frosts. They are great for cut flowers. Lilies and gladioli can go in now.

In containers

- Choose a pot deep enough for the bulb to sit at its correct planting depth.
- Place broken pot 'crocks' at the bottom of the pots to aid drainage.
- Place a layer of multipurpose compost with added grit into the pot base.
- Generally, bulbs (and this dahlia tuber) should be set at three times their depth.
- Sit bulbs with their shoots upwards.
- Cover the bulbs with compost, and water. Apply a high potash feed when growth is seen.

In the ground

- Plant in groups for a stunning border display.
- As a rough guide, the planting hole should be double the size of the bulb.
- If planting bulbs for cut flowers, such as gladioli, dig a trench and plant in staggered rows.
- Always plant them nose or shoot upwards.
- Cover with soil and gently firm down with the back of a rake.
- Mark the area so you are aware of where they are planted, thus avoiding treading on and damaging young growth.

SIX SUMMER BULBS TO GROW

Freesia: These are tender corms, and they do well in pots. Plant the corms 1-2in (2.5-5cm) deep and 3-4in (7.5-9cm) apart.

Tigridia: If planting outside choose a south or west facing bed. Wait until the risk of frosts has passed to plant outdoors, or plant in containers in greenhouse or coldframe. Plant 2in (5cm) deep and 6in (15cm) apart.

Homeria: These grow well in sandy soil. Plant 1-2in (2.5-5cm) deep in groups, or use as a 'filler'.

Gladiolus: Plant in an open, sunny site for the best flowers until late spring. Plant at a depth of about 3in (7.5cm), and 8in (20cm) apart.

Lily: These bulbs appreciate leaf mould added to the planting hole to help keep their roots cool. Plant 6in (15cm) deep and 12in (30cm) apart.

Dahlia: For early flowering, start dahlias off in moist compost in boxes protected from frosts, and then plant out in late spring. If planting directly outdoors, do it after the last frost, at a depth of about 4-6in (10-15cm).

POTS OF COLOUR FOR SUMMER

Get patios and decking set for summer with bedding baskets and containers.

If you have a greenhouse, conservatory, porch or large windowsill, you can plant up your summer pots and harden the plants off in their final containers – as long as pots are light enough to move. If not, or you don't have space under cover, hold off for a week or two before planting up.

If you grow your own bedding plants, by late spring they should be ready for use.

Tender perennials like petunia, verbena, geranium and fuchsia are common options but seek out some more unusual varieties, and don't forget hardy annuals either.

Whether you want to stock your patios or decking with stunning colour in containers, or add colour at height with hanging baskets, use these simple steps to planting, for success with summer bedding this season.

QUICK TIP

If you've got lots of pots to plant, get the boring bit done first and fill them all with compost before you start planting.

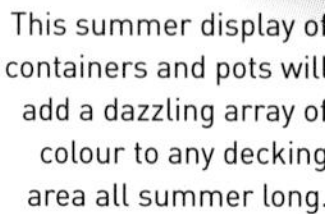

This summer display of containers and pots will add a dazzling array of colour to any decking area all summer long.

STEP BY STEP Summer hanging baskets

1. Pierce plastic liners for drainage –moss, coir, felt liners etc, need no cutting. Add water crystals and slow-release fertiliser to multipurpose compost and part fill the basket.

2. It can be difficult to fill around plants in the confines of a basket. As an alternative, remove plants from their pots, space the pots in the basket and fill around them with compost.

10 TIPS FOR TOP POTS

- Add water retaining crystals to help plants cope with summer extremes. Also add slow release fertiliser to compost at planting time or use liquid feeds through the season.
- Try a branded container and basket compost. Theses have added fertiliser and moisture retention technology, cutting down on the need to water and feed.
- Pinch out early flowers on newly planted bedding, this will divert growth to roots and shoots, boosting establishment.
- When using porous terracotta pots, sink planted plastic containers inside to reduce watering needs or line the terracotta pots with compost bags before planting up.
- Include taller centrepiece plants to add structure and height to container displays. Good options include annual climbers, cordylines, cannas, lilies and small evergreen shrubs.
- For something different add the odd tomato plant or other tender greenhouse vegetable like pepper, chilli and aubergine to your pot displays.
- Never let compost dry out. Allowing plants to wilt in between watering checks growth and reduces plant vigour.
- Link multiple pots with a running theme. Either use the same colour scheme in each pot or repeat one variety in each.

- At the start of the season, water pots early in the day, so foliage can dry ahead of colder night temperatures. Later in the season water in the evening to prevent sun scorch on wet leaves during the day.

- If taking a summer holiday, move pots to a shady corner of the garden, remove all flowers and buds, and water well before setting off.

3.

Remove the empty pots one at a time to drop in the plants, pinching around the rootball to firm in. Use trailing or semi-trailing plants around the edges. Choose upright plants for the centre.

4.

Water well to settle in. To harden off, keep your basket outside on warm days, but bring it under cover each evening. To keep upright while inside, set them in bucket or large pot.

MID-SUMMER ESSENTIALS

Make time for some of the smaller but none-the-less important jobs that can fall by the wayside as you sit back to enjoy the garden.

Control weed growth

Mid-summer is the time to start enjoying all your hard work. If you do little else to keep the garden ticking over, you must spend some time tackling weed growth.

Regular hoeing will remove the need to get down on hands and knees to pull established weeds by hand. It is surprising and gratifying to see how much weed growth can be lifted if you set aside an hour or so to tackle them.

Where weeds have crept into the joins in paths, patios and drives a weeding knife or hook works well in scraping away green growth. To stop regrowth on hard surfaces, areas can be treated with a residual weedkiller which will prevent weeds growing back for up to six months. Systemic weedkillers can also be used to spot spray established weeds elsewhere in the garden. Just be sure to avoid wetting the foliage of prized garden plants.

Keep greenhouses cool

Level extreme temperatures in the greenhouse by opening doors and windows each morning, and damp down all hard surface to raise humidity. Shade netting will also help to keep temperatures down.

Love your lawn

Give the lawn a fast-acting, high-nitrogen summer feed, especially if you didn't feed it in spring. Mow regularly, but during hot, dry spells, raise the blades to reduce stress on the turf.

Hedge maintenance

Clip and shape evergreen hedges such as privet, box and the small-leaved hedging honeysuckle with shears or a powered hedge cutter.

Large-leaved varieties, such as laurel, should be cut with secateurs to avoid leaving ragged, cut leaves on the hedge. For a straight, flat finish run a string along the side and top of the hedge and don't cut in past this point.

Keep the veg patch productive

Keep repeat croppers cropping by regularly picking fruit. Courgettes and cucumbers need particular attention. Cucumbers will stop if fruit is left too long, and courgettes will quickly turn to marrows if not picked. Where space is available sow main crop carrots, as well as peas, spring cabbage, turnips, French beans and beetroot for continued cropping.

Keep ponds in condition

Keep ponds oxygenated by clearing algae, blanket weed and debris. When removing pond plants, leave them at the water's edge for 24 hours to allow pond life the chance to get back in the water. Better still, lay mesh across the pond and sit the debris on this, so creatures can drop back down into the water. Adding a fountain will help to oxygenate the water, too.

Dave Bevan

Support tall perennials

Stake tall border flowers, such as dahlia and delphinium, and even foxglove, lupin and kniphofia in exposed gardens, to keep them looking their best. Wind and rain can cause stems to bend, but even in sheltered spots, the weight of flowering spikes can cause them to buckle. Even shorter plants with flower spikes will benefit from this.

Graham Clarke

Watch out for pests and diseases

Cabbage white butterflies will be laying eggs. Aphids (green and blackfly) will be seeking out fresh stem growth, and summer rain can bring in blight on tomato and potato crops.

Net brassicas against cabbage whites. Spray plants with soap spray or insecticide to protect against aphids.

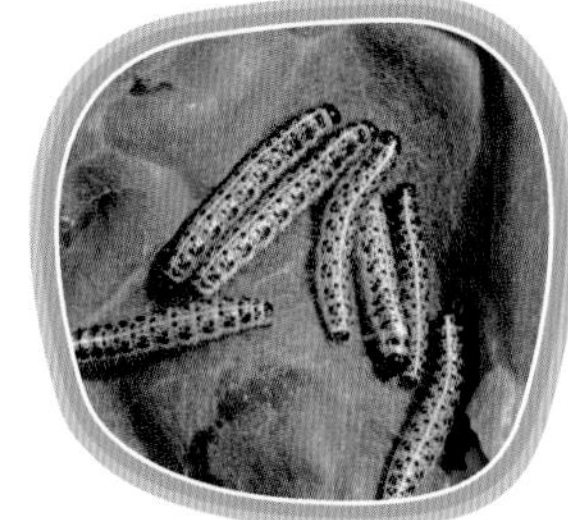

Pots and baskets

Keep containers and baskets well watered, this may need to be done daily – even twice a day– during very hot weather.

Offer pot plants a fast acting liquid or soluble feed once a week to keep them in healthy growth.

While watering and feeding, check plants for faded blooms, and remove these to encourage rapid re-growth, and more floral colour in your displays.

Take soft wood/stem tip cuttings

A wide range of shrubs, perennials and bedding plants can be propagated this way. Take 4in (10cm) cuttings from bedding and perennials. Remove the lower leaves and growing tip keeping a pair of leaves, then set several cuttings around an 8in (20cm) pot filled with cuttings compost. Take 6-8in (15-20cm) lengths from shrubby plants and treat in the same manner.

AUTUMN BEDDING

Get your cooler season bedding sown.

One confusion of gardening comes with the term 'autumn bedding'. It actually normally refers to 'spring bedding' or even 'winter bedding'. They're all the same!

You see, when talking about autumn bedding we are really meaning the bedding that is planted in autumn, aiming for a floral display in spring. These cold hardy plants may flower over winter, and if sown now will most likely give a flush of colour at planting time, before colder weather puts them in check until spring. You can see how the confusion has arisen.

Young plants will grow over the summer, to be at the perfect size for autumn planting.

Though treated as annuals, mostly these plants are biennial (which are sown and germinate one year, then grow, flower and die the next year). Sometimes they are short-lived perennials (violas and primroses).

Sowing them indoors is normal practice, but they are hardy, so can also be sown outside. Choose an area for a seedbed, in full or part sun. Dig over the soil and remove weeds, then firm and rake the area to form a fine tilth. Sow your chosen seeds into a ¼in (6mm) deep drill. They should germinate within six weeks.

STEP BY STEP Indoor sowing of autumn bedding

Fill a seed or module tray with a good quality seed compost. Tap it on to a flat surface to evenly level the medium. Then water it well.

Sow the seeds of your chosen variety over the surface of the compost – evenly and thinly. You can do this straight from the packet.

Cover with a ¼ in (6mm) layer of vermiculite or sieved compost. Fine seeds, such as foxgloves, should not be covered. Don't forget to label.

10 AUTUMN BEDDING PLANTS TO SOW NOW

- Brompton stock (*Matthiola bicornis*)
- Cyclamen (*Cyclamen persicum*)
- Double daisy (*Bellis perennis*)
- Bugle (*Ajuga reptans*)
- Persian buttercup (*Ranunculus asiaticus*)
- Ornamental kale (*Brassica oleracea*)
- Pansies and violas (*Viola*)
- Primroses and polyanthus (*Primula*)
- Sweet William (*Dianthus barbatus*)
- Wallflower (*Cheiranthus cheiri*)

NOTES:

QUICK TIP

If sown early, some types of bedding (including pansies, dasies and primroses) may produce autumn blooms.

AUTUMN LAWN CARE

The timely jobs we should all be doing to our lawns in autumn.

Although it is cooler in autumn, the lawn is still growing – usually when temperatures reach 5°C (41°F) or higher – so mowing is necessary.

Early autumn is – or should be – a busy time in terms of lawn care. The routine is: scarify, aerate, topdress… in that order. Use an autumn feed if necessary and repair areas (ie. rebuilding collapsed lawn edges, removing bumps and hollows and re-seeding bald spots).

Feeding

An autumn feed isn't always necessary, but if your lawn has suffered from summer's dry and hot weather, it's worth applying a feed. Only use an autumn feed – that is, one higher in phosphorous and potash, and lower in nitrogen. It will encourage 'harder' growth, better able to withstand winter temperatures. Look for feeds with added weed and mosskiller.

STEP BY STEP

One way to improve the look of your lawn is to repair any damaged edges:

Using a spade, cut three sides of a square of turf that includes the damaged or broken edge.

Gently undercut the turf. Lift it, then turn it so that the broken edge is facing in to the lawn.

Drop the reversed turf back into the same position, lightly firming into place with your foot.

1.

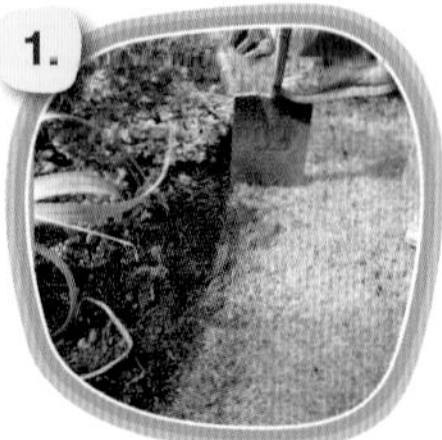

2.

3.

Scarifying

This is best done in autumn (you can 'spot' scarify heavily mossy areas of the lawn in spring, but if you do the whole lawn then you risk setting it back for the whole summer). Tug a spring-tine rake (or a powered scarifier) across the grass so that the tines repeatedly pull at the tangled mass of grass. This removes thatch and moss from the lawn surface, and gives the grass breathing space and room to fill out and create a dense sward.

Aerating

If a lawn isn't aerated every year, it will suffer from compaction. This expels airs from between the soil particles, which means that the grass roots cannot gain access to moisture and nutrients. Grass becomes sparse and stunted. So aerating, once a year (after scarifying), is important. A way to do this is to use a garden fork to spike the lawn to a depth of 4-6in (10-15cm). A hollow-tine aerator may prove better on heavy soils.

Topdressing

Applying topsoil to an aerated lawn loosely fills the holes and any minor hollows, and it encourages the grass to produce more roots and runners. When a loamy mix is used on sandy soil it can improve its water-retaining potential, whilst a sandy topdressing on a heavy soil can help to improve drainage. Mixing a topdressing is easy – here are the best recipes:

For a heavy soil, mix 1 part multipurpose compost, 2 parts loam and 4 parts sand. For a loamy soil, mix 1 part multipurpose compost, 4 parts loam and 2 parts sand. For a light soil, mix 2 parts multipurpose compost, 4 parts loam and 1 part sand. Apply small heaps across the lawn, and use a besom broom or the back of a rake to ease it into the aeration holes, as well as any shallow hollows in the lawn surface.

Sweeping

If there are tall deciduous trees within the vicinity, it can be guaranteed that their fallen autumn leaves will be covering areas of your lawn. Don't let these leaves stay in place for more than a few days, otherwise the grass underneath will really suffer.

To make sure that the edges merge into the existing lawn, firm them into place with your fingers.

If there are any gaps between the turf and the lawn, fill with sieved soil mixed with a little grass seed.

Bang the turf into place with the back of a spade: this levels it, and expels any air pockets under it.

Sweep the area to make it tidy. After a few days, create the new edge with a half moon cutter.

4.

5.

6.

7.

TEN AUTUMN ESSENTIALS

With misty days and leaves starting to carpet the ground, here are ten important jobs that need to be done once autumn arrives.

Autumn planting

Autumn is the best time of the year for planting hardy perennials, trees and shrubs. For these subjects, winter cold does not affect them adversely as it is the time when they are dormant. Planting them now, whilst the soil is still warm from summer, and made moist from the autumn rains, means that they will set news roots in the soil and become established before the onset of winter. The alternative season for planting is spring, but many expert gardeners maintain that when planted then, the plants do not have a long-enough time to establish before they are expected to put on their summer foliage, flower and/or fruiting displays.

Strawberry bed clear-up

Remove any old runners, dead or yellowing foliage, and old fruiting stalks from established strawberry plants. Also, 'tickle' over the soil with a border fork (gently turning the top inch or two), and weed the area to tidy it up and lessen the risk of pest and disease problems next year.

Any older plants showing signs of virus infection (mottling or stunting of the foliage) should be taken out and disposed of – do not put these on the compost heap.

Transplant evergreens

Apart from planting trees, shrubs and perennials, this is the perfect time to transplant those evergreen trees or shrubs that are growing in the wrong place. With a full canopy of leaves, transplanting in moist autumn soil means that there is less need to apply masses of water in order to help establishment of the roots.

If your garden is exposed to the wind, it would be a good idea to but up a wind shelter on the windward side of the plant, to prevent the leaves from drying out.

Plant out spring cabbages

Rake the soil level before planting, and ensure that it is firm but not compacted. Set them 6in (15cm) apart in rows that are 12in (30cm) apart. Do not feed spring cabbages after planting as this encourages soft growth – and most of the nutrients will be washed away by winter rains anyway.

Greenhouse tasks

Clean down the staging and brush up any soil or compost from shelves. Also, give the glazing a good clean, as it is important to allow as much winter light as possible into the house.

Buy and put up bubble wrap to insulate the greenhouse. Go for the biggest 'bubbles' you can get; these allow best light transmission. It may cost a few pounds to buy the wrap, but it is likely to save much more in reducing your heating bills.

Dig empty areas of soil

Unless you've adopted the 'no-dig' system, it is a good idea to dig over any areas of the veg plot (or any other bed or border) as soon as they are cleared. The sooner soil cultivation can be done the better. Heavy, or clay soils in particular will benefit from being broken up and exposed to winter weather conditions for as long as possible.

Frost and snow both play a vital part in breaking down soil particles, enabling you to make better planting and seed beds in the spring.

Lift and store gladioli

Gladioli leaves have started to go yellow, so lift the corms before they are damaged by frost. Lift with a fork, leaving the foliage until it has dried off. Then twist it off and dust the corms with sulphur to prevent disease getting in. Keep them dry and frostfree over winter.

Clear gutters of leaves

Most of us tend to remember to sweep up autumn leaves from patios and driveways, and many of us remember to sweep them up from lawns (because if left they can harm the grass). But most of us tend to forget to remove leaves that have collected in gutters and drains, and this is important if you want to avoid bad blockages or nasty stinks!

Clear fallen leaves from beds and borders, too, and especially from rockeries where the delicate alpine plants can quickly rot under a wet covering of leaves.

Reduce feeding fish

As the days get shorter and cooler, pond fish become less active, and therefore eat less food. Reduce the amount you give them; just give a small pinch. If it is eaten give a little more; if it is not, give less next time. Any food not eaten will decompose in the water, and too much of this will turn the water toxic, and fish and wildlife will suffer.

Prune climbing roses

Now that the summer flowers on climbing roses have finished, it is time to prune the plants. It is important to do this soon, and to get the retained branches tied in, before autumn winds pick up (as these can snap off the stiff stems). Follow this by clearing up the fallen leaves from around the bottom of the plant; these can harbour diseases such as blackspot.

Discard or burn these leaves rather than add them to the compost heap.

WINTER LAWN REPAIRS

Use mild days in winter to carry out simple lawn repairs and maintenance.

Scarifying

Deeply raking the lawn's surface allows air to get to the grass roots. Normally a job for spring or autumn, it is often only in mid-winter when you can see the mass of thatch (dead grass and debris) that builds up, which can stifle new growth. If your lawn is mossy, don't scarify now; wait until mid-spring or autumn, and do it about two weeks after you have treated the area with a mosskiller.

1.

Aeration

A compacted lawn means that the grass is weak. In severe cases it may die completely, resulting in bare patches. So, if winter puddles form on the lawn, waste no time in aerating the area by spiking. Drive a garden fork into the soil so that the tines penetrate to a depth of 3in (7cm). Do this over the whole lawn if you can manage it – but at least tackle the areas most affected by pooling water.

2.

Repairs

Repair broken or worn edges. Here Use a powered trimmer to redefine the edge of an overgrown border. For a crisp, deep edge use a half moon cutter. Level bumps in the lawn by lifting turf and removing soil beneath, before relaying the turf. Fill in hollows by lifting turf and building up the soil level beneath.

3.

Worm casts

Worms are welcome, but those species that produce casts cause problems. The casts contain weed seeds, and if you walk over and flatten them they kill off the grass underneath. Remove the casts by sweeping them with a broom.

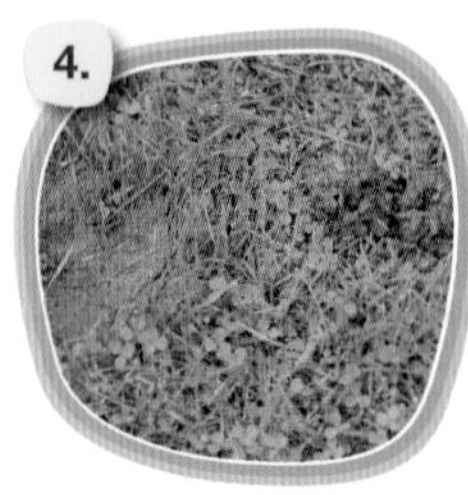
4.

Snowmould

This fungal disease occurs in winter on moist soils where grass is compacted. It starts as a patch of yellow grass, that turns brown and dies. Cotton-like fungal growth around the edge of the patch gives the disease its name. Apply fungicide, following the instructions. In spring, aerate and scarify the lawn to improve drainage.

5.

Frosty lawns

Finally, never walk on the grass when it is frozen or excessively muddy. In the case of frost, you will kill the grass in foot-shaped marks. With muddy soil the grass plants get squished into the mud and the lawn will take a long time to recover.

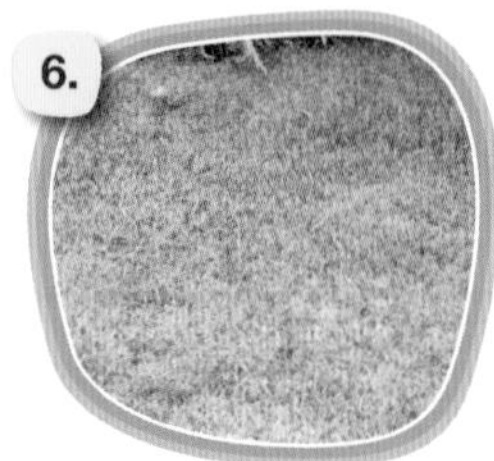
6.

FILLING GAPPY HEDGES

How to rectify the problem of a hedge with dead patches.

Gaps can sometimes form in hedges, due to the weather or just the age of the shrubs. To replace a whole hedge can be costly – and takes a long time – so it makes sense to fill the gaps with 'whips' (2 or 3-year-old bare-rooted plants). Ideally, use the same species as the hedge.

Replacing the section with new plants sounds simple, but they will need extra care – they have to fight for light and nutrients against their bigger neighbours.

Now is a good time to do this. But you should only plant if the soil is workable – neither frozen nor waterlogged. If it is, heel in the whips and plant them properly when the soil is in a better state.

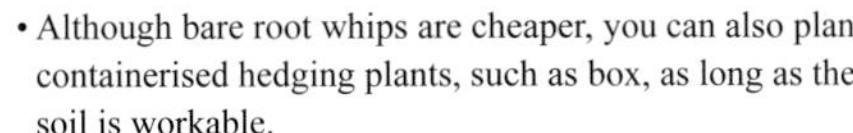

- Although bare root whips are cheaper, you can also plant containerised hedging plants, such as box, as long as the soil is workable.

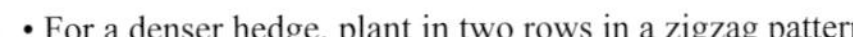

- For a denser hedge, plant in two rows in a zigzag pattern.
- Planting distances will vary depending on what variety you plant. As a rule set plants 12-24in (30-60cm) apart.
- Before planting soak the whips for 30 minutes in a pail of water.
- Dig a trench and add well-rotted manure or compost.
- Place whips in position and spread the roots, backfill the soil and gently firm in with your foot.
- Once planted, water and mulch with bark chippings. Place tree guards around them if they are at risk of mammals nibbling them.
- Feed in spring and summer with bonemeal or growmore at 4oz per sq yd (140g per sq m).

POT PLANT PERSISTENCE

Here's what to do with Christmas plants that are starting to fade.

It seems a shame to throw all these away when they stop being colourful.

After Christmas, pot plants will be fading. Some are going into a resting period, which is quite normal. The bulbs – paperwhites, hyacinths and amaryllis – all need to convert energy from their leaves, into stored nutrients within the bulb so they can flower again the following year.

Winter cherry, cyclamen and poinsettias take a rest during the spring and summer and put energy into forming new buds or stems.

It seems a shame to even contemplate throwing away any of these plants. With some care, it is quite possible to keep them going, and allow them to give another burst of colour.

If you can't look after them all, which should you choose to save? It's down to personal choice really, but some are rather more conducive to repeat flowering than others.

QUICK TIP

Pot azaleas are not hardy to start with! After Christmas indoors, harden them off before planting outside.

Hyacinths

Once your hyacinth bulbs have finished flowering and the flower stems have withered, cut them off at the base. Leave the foliage to replenish the bulb with energy. Feed fortnightly with a liquid, all-purpose fertiliser until the leaves die down. Remove the foliage, and plant the bulbs outside in the soil to grow naturally for next year.

Cyclamen

With indoor cyclamen, wait until they stop flowering, then reduce watering and stop feeding. Place in a cool, well-lit room until the spring, when they can be placed outside or in a greenhouse. Re-pot in summer with fresh compost, keeping them moist throughout summer. Bring back indoors before the temperature drops in autumn.

Azalea

Remove the dead flowers and move plants to a cool room over late winter to encourage new buds to form. Feed weekly with a liquid fertiliser, high in potassium (such as tomato feed). Place outside in a shady spot for summer. Sink the pot into the ground to stop them drying out, and bring back indoors before the first frosts.

Potting on long-term plants

Many plants, such as azaleas and winter cherry, like to be snug in their pots. Pot them on only if roots are seen coming from the bottom of the pot, and when growth starts after their resting period. Look for new buds and leaf growth to indicate the plant is coming back to life.

Repot only one pot size up; pots that are too big run the risk of making the plant divert its energy into making new roots and not into flower or leaf production.

In the case of the winter cherry, prune the branches back by half; then sit the pot outside in a shady spot.

Azaleas need to be given ericaceous compost. Most other plants will be happy in multipurpose compost.

Should you keep all of them?

Some plants should be treated as temporary, like a vase of cut flowers. By all means keep those you like, but not to the point where your summer plants may get forgotten.

Remember that from early autumn, poinsettias need 14 hours of darkness and 10 hours of daylight to form their colourful bracts.

Note also that forced bulbs rarely flower the next year if forced again, as they have little time to regain their energy. Instead, plant them outside so they can revert to their normal growth.

Finally, if you do consign plants to the compost heap, don't feel guilty about it: the cost of keeping them going may be greater than buying a new one!

Poinsettias

These are difficult: they'll lose their red bracts, leaving just the green foliage. After leaf fall, cut stems back to a healthy bud and let the plants rest, keeping them almost dry. Place on a tray with wet pebbles to maintain humidity, spray new foliage daily with clean water. Repot the plants in early summer, and feed with a general liquid houseplant fertiliser.

Amaryllis

Remove the faded flowers then allow the stem to die back before removing it at the base. Leave an inch or so of stalk – be careful not to damage the growing point at the top of the bulb. Until autumn, water and feed weekly, using a balanced liquid feed. Place the bulbs, in their pots, outside in a shady position after the last frosts of late spring.

Paperwhite narcissi

These bulbs are not hardy, and won't grow well if planted outdoors. When they stop flowering, remove the faded blooms, and let the stem and leaves turn yellow. To flower again the leaves need to wither for six weeks or so (to feed nutrients back to the bulb). Keep outside in the shade over summer and bring back indoors before the first frosts.

CHRISTMAS POT REVAMP

The season is long gone, but your festive pots could still be in colour. Time for a change...

Some Christmas plants are still full of vigour within. If you have Christmas displays still lurking in the garden, use the tips here to rehome the plants and keep them going through spring.

New additions

Spring bedding is still widely available at this time of year, as are spring bulbs 'in the green' and evergreen dot plants such as euonymus, mini conifers and ivy. If you need a few more plants to finish the look, add yellow rose-bud primroses and some white hyacinths to the display to freshen it and move away from the red colour scheme that just shouted 'Christmas'.

Plant maintenance

If you've been a bit relaxed with the upkeep of your Christmas pots, give the plants a thorough inspection before deciding to keep them. Look for signs of rots and moulds – it should be possible to remove the infected material, hoping that new growth will remain healthy – spray with a plant fungicide as an extra precaution. Also remove all faded flower heads and spent foliage. Do this before the plants are moved.

Pots: old for new

With months still to go before the threat of frost is over, your replacements need to be frostproof. If you are going to repot into terracotta containers, make sure they will withstand cold spells. If unsure, opt for wooden, plastic or metal pots. To keep your festive pots for re-use next Christmas, wipe down with a damp sponge inside and out, set out to dry, then store in the shed or garage.

Feeding for flowers

Bedding plants don't usually need feeding in winter. But if it's been particularly wet, nutrients will have been washed through pot compost. To ensure plenty of flowers until early summer it's worth offering plants a feed now. A liquid feed will offer a fast fix, but if more rain is to follow a granular slow release option may be better.

DECKING DEEP CLEAN

Winter rain and a build-up of algae can make your decking a no-go area. Here's how to bring it back in use.

There are many no-effort cleaning liquids on the market – simply apply to your decking and leave to dry, but these are best saved for lighter work. For a really deep clean, pressure washing is the best option. This is a tedious task and one that requires some dedication if you are to be left with an evenly clean surface. To avoid rushing the job and leaving zigzag lines over the area, mentally divide the decking area into manageable sections and do the job in small doses over a period of time.

QUICK TIP

Get a quote from a local tradesman before carrying out the job yourself – a good quote may outweigh your time and effort.

Before...

After...

Jet wash cleaning

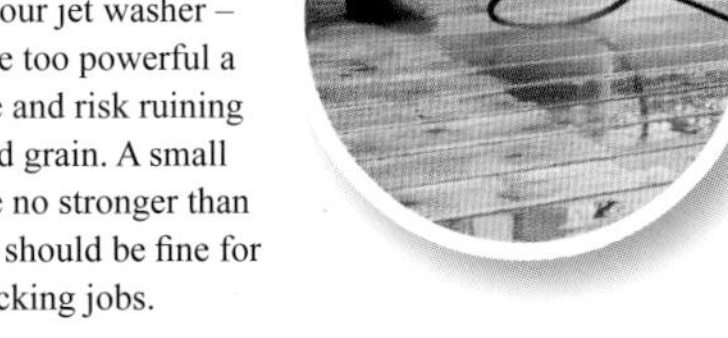

- Use a stiff-bristled broom to thoroughly brush away all loose grime and debris such as fallen leaves.
- Set up your jet washer – don't use too powerful a machine and risk ruining the wood grain. A small machine no stronger than 1500psi should be fine for most decking jobs.
- Where possible, clean a plank at a time, from one end to the other, for an even finish.
- If your decking is attached to a building, work from the building out, so water is pushed away from foundations.

Lasting effect

- To lighten old wood once clean, apply a weak citric acid or hydrogen peroxide solution.
- Use a decking fungicide across the area while it is still slightly damp.
- If you have surplus plant fungicides in the shed these can be applied as an alternative.
- Over the season, sweep the deck regularly to prevent a buildup of debris. If water sits on the deck after heavy rain, sweep this away.
- Later in the year, during good weather and when the deck is fully dry, apply a decking oil, stain or preserver.

GREEN FINGER TIPS

DIFFERENT WAYS TO SOW

Different types of containers for sowing seeds, and their advantages.

Your free seeds are back, which means only one thing – sowing season is upon us.

It's still early doors for seed sowing- in late winter it's best to concentrate on seeds that need extra heat before moving on to the bulk of sowing in spring. If you're not stocked up on compost, propagators and pots, don't fret. The guide here will show you some of the best options to get you started.

As in any hobby it's easy to get carried away on kitting yourself out with the right products for the job. It's nice to have quality products to hand but as my money-saving tips show, it's possible to sow and grow for the price of your seeds and some quality seed compost.

When you want to grow lots of one type of plant, an open seed tray is the best choice for a spacing-saving sowing container.

FIVE OF THE BEST

Choose one or more of these containers to get your sowing started

• Seed trays

A traditional option allowing tens, even hundreds, of seeds to be sown in one quick batch. All seedlings will require pricking out and potting on.

• Cell trays

Modular trays for sowing a few seeds per cell. No pricking out is needed, the weakest seedlings are pinched out to leave one to grow on as a plug plant.

• Root trainers

Similar to cell trays but allowing deep root development. No pricking out is needed. The trainers open out to reveal the root balls, causing minimal disturbance when potting on.

LITTLE AND OFTEN GETS THE JOB DONE

It's easy to get carried away with sowing, but there's no point in filling all available windowsill or greenhouse space with pots and trays full of seed – the seedlings will soon need pricking out and potting on, and finding a suitable spot to grow them on successfully becomes a problem.

If you rely on the windowsill to get your plants started, or only have limited greenhouse space, sow a few small batches every week through spring. Not only will this reduce demand for indoor growing space, it will break up the time spent on pricking out the young seedlings.

For sowing in small batches, use a heated propagator, which houses seven mini propagator trays.

A low-cost alternative for this is to sow small numbers of seed in small pots and set each pot in it's own clear plastic bag to keep them warm enough to germinate.

QUICK TIP

When sowing little and often, never forget to label each sowing container, it's easy to get confused.

Starting seed for free

Have a look through your recyclables before you take them out to the bin for collection. So many packaging items can be adapted for seed sowing. Any plastic food packaging tray that will hold 2in (5cm) of compost can be used as a no cost seed tray – just remember to pierce a few drainage holes in the bottom. Yoghurt pots, sauce pots, toilet rolls – even tin cans (watch for sharp edges) are all suitable subjects.

Make use of those free papers that come through the door each week, too. Rather than drop them straight into the recycling bin, treat yourself to a paper plant pot maker and make your own little pots for sowing.

4.

• Cell trays

Modular trays for sowing a few seeds per cell. No pricking out is needed, the weakest seedlings are pinched out to leave one to grow on as a plug plant.

5.

• Root trainers

Similar to cell trays but allowing deep root development. No pricking out is needed. The trainers open out to reveal the root balls, causing minimal disturbance when potting on.

FIX WEATHER DAMAGE

How to fix problems caused by frost and rain.

Garden plants come to little harm when hit by short-lived flash floods after heavy rain, and the majority (if sensibly chosen) will cope with short periods of snow cover and heavy frost.

However, prolonged spells of saturated soil and freezing temperatures will take their toll in many gardens.

QUICK TIP

Yellowing leaves are a sign of waterlog damage, while brown 'burnt' foliage is a sure sign of frost damage.

Is your shed in sound condition? After periods of heavy rain, leaking shed roofs will be easy to spot. If wet patches are evident inside your shed, it's time to re-felt the roof.

Have certain areas remained saturated all winter?

Improve drainage, or replant the area with plants that cope well in damp conditions – a bog garden may be the answer, or raised beds may help.

Are my drains coping with the rain?

Ahead of heavy rain, sweep all surfaces and collect debris that may be washed into drains. If already blocked, get someone in to flush the drain or hire a drain rod set and give it a go yourself.

Are plants yellowing or turning brown?

Yellowing plants after a wet season are a sign of waterlogging. Brown 'burnt' foliage after a cold snap is a sign of frost damage. Cut back affected growth to healthy stem and buds. Fork the soil around yellowing plants, adding grit or compost to the area. Feed with a balanced fertiliser in spring and mulch around bases. A foliar feed in spring can re-colour yellow foliage. Only prune frost hit stems once all threat of frost has past.

Do my boundaries create a frost pocket?

Think about opening up gaps in the lowest lying boundary line, to allow cold air to pass through rather than sinking and sitting against it. This will reduce the risk of prolonged frost.

Has frost lifted new trees and shrubs out of the soil?

Use your heel to firm them back into the ground once defrosted. Take care not to damage the main stem.

Has my lawn over winter?

Spike the lawn to alleviate compaction. If this is a regular occurrence, think about digging out a seasonal pond at the lowest point of the garden where runoff can collect. In severe cases slit drainage (a narrow trench filled with sand or gravel) may be needed to divert water away.

Are planting beds waterlogged?

Add grit or gravel and plenty of compost to soils to improve drainage. Alternatively site raised beds on the area to set plants above the water table.

Did my pond overflow or stay frozen for a length of time?

Prevent fish and plant losses by adding an overflow pipe to the pond. Attach mesh over the inlet and place the outlet into a drain. Alternatively dig out a soakaway next to the pond where excess water spills out. During freezing temperatures add a floating heater or ball to the surface to keep a breathing hole open.

Are my sheds and structures in sound condition?

Check inside for signs of leaks, replace planks if needed and re-felt roofing if water damage is seen.

Has my veg patch sat in flood water?

Avoid eating ready-to-eat crops, particularly roots, as flood water may have carried pollutants such as sewage onto the site.

Has my water butt been overflowing?

If yours has overflowed this winter, buy a return pipe kit and add it to the set up so that excess water is returned to the down pipe and into drains.

Have my pot plants become waterlogged?

Raise pots onto feet to create better drainage. Pour excess water out of waterlogged pots and think about repotting plants into fresh compost in severe cases. Move pots to sheltered areas of the garden.

FEEDING SOILS

Choosing the right fertiliser will get your plants off to a good start.

Fertilisers are a concentrated source of nutrients that can be applied to nearly all garden plants and vegetables. Applying them during winter gives plants the nutrients they need for spring growth.

Fertilisers are essential for putting back nutrition that has either been used up by established plants or leached out during the winter. They are best applied as a base dressing (mixed into the soil), or as a top dressing (applied to the surface of the soil).

Follow the instructions on how much fertiliser to use. If you have already dug in organic matter this winter you will need to apply just a little fertiliser. It is possible to overfeed, and this can harm the plant.

Feeding the plant now with fish, blood and bone will help the developing fruiting buds.

Below are the best types of fertiliser to use in different areas of the garden.

Trees and shrubs

Late winter and early spring are the best times to feed trees, shrubs and hedges. Unless your soil is impoverished, they need feeding only once a year.

Apply as a base or top dressing, but don't let the feed touch the main trunk or stems, as this may damage or scorch the wood.

Lawn care

Grass grows rapidly as soon as the soil temperature reaches 5°C (41°F). To aid healthy growth, spread chicken manure pellets or sulphate of ammonia evenly on lawns. There are many lawn feeds available, some with selective weedkillers, but these can be expensive and may overfeed the grass at this time of year.

Vegetables

Although vegetables need nutrients to grow well, if plenty of organic matter (such as compost) was dug in late last year, reduce the amount of fertiliser you add. Apply chicken pellets. Brassicas are very hungry plants and a helping of nitrogen-rich sulphate of ammonia will boost leaf growth.

GET TO KNOW YOUR SOILS

Understanding your soil is the first step towards growing healthy, strong plants. If you have been struggling to grow decent plants, or you want to grow something new, it is wise to test the nutrient levels and pH value of the soil. (This is a measurement of whether your soil is acidic or alkaline).

Your soil's pH level will have a major influence on what plants will grow well in the garden. In general, most plants like a pH of 6.5-7.0; in this range they can easily obtain nutrients from the soil. Kits are readily available from garden centres or online. Make sure you get the most value from a soil-testing kit, by using it properly:

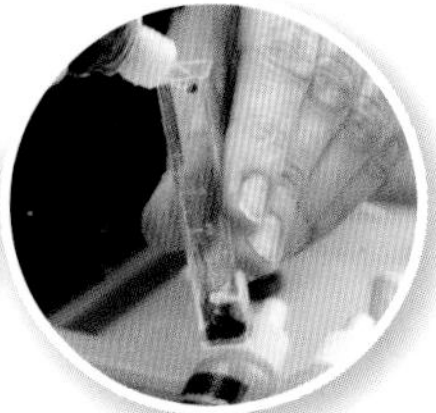

• Choose a kit that enables you to check all the major nutrients. Nitrogen is essential to all plants, but too much can damage them. Phosphorus is needed for strong root growth, and potassium/potash for improved flowers.

• When testing for nutrients or pH levels always use soil at least 2in (5cm) below the surface, for a more accurate test. Whilst collecting soil, do not touch it with bare hands; chemicals on the skin may affect results.

• It is important to test different areas of the garden: natural leaching of nutrients, the weather, and the decomposition of plants can all change the nutrient levels of soil. Keep a record of where you collected the soil samples.

• Soil testing is a great way to make gardening more appealing to older children, and it will help them with their science key stages.

Containers

All containerised plants will need a feed in spring; the soil in the containers will be lacking in nutrients. It is wise to scrape away the top layer of soil and add fresh compost to the display before feeding. Use a controlled release fertiliser, which will feed for about six months. In summer use a liquid feed.

Blooming flowers

Some perennial plants and annuals do not need to be fed at all (such as wild flowers). But some, like sweet peas, can soon use up nutrients in the soil.

Give them a kick-start by sprinkling fish, blood and bone around the bases, or mix into the soil before planting. This will help flowering.

Edible fruits

Fruiting trees and bushes benefit from a feed in early spring to aid bud and fruit development. Sulphate of potash or fish, blood and bone will help. Culinary apples require a balanced feed to encourage leafy growth. Use chicken pellets as an organic option.

GREENHOUSE PREPARATION

Get your greenhouse ready for the growing season ahead.

With light levels and temperatures increasing, early spring is the time to prepare greenhouses for the new growing season.

If you use your greenhouse to care for seedlings, or grow heat-loving plants, vegetables or fruits, there are some timely tasks that need to be done to keep them all healthy and happy.

QUICK TIP

Invest in a greenhouse thermometer to monitor major drops and rapid rises in heat, which may affect plants.

Increase light

Dirty windows will affect the amount of light that reaches the plants inside the greenhouse; they need as much light as possible for strong plant growth. Washing the glass and frames will remove any fungal growth or pests that may have overwintered in the framework.

On a mild, sunny day using hot, soapy water, wash the windows inside and out, clean between vents and openings and leave the door open to allow the glass to dry quickly.

Improve humidity

Most plants and seedlings like a higher humidity level in which to grow; dry air causes them to lose moisture quickly (which can lead to poor growth as they use all their energy to retain valuable moisture). Increase humidity by damping down staging and floors with a hose or watering can. Place a tray of water on the floor so it slowly evaporates into the air.

Pest control

The increase in heat in greenhouses makes it the perfect place for pests to breed. Put up sticky traps to catch flying pests, check under pots and staging for slugs and snails. If there is a major build-up of pests, use a greenhouse fumigator, but if using a chemical-based one, remove all plant material before using.

WATERING IDEAS

As seedlings and plants grow at speed in spring, they will need more water. There are many things you can do to make watering in the greenhouse easier. Follow these ideas:

- Attach a water butt to the greenhouse to save time running backwards and forward to the house (where water butts are mostly fitted).
- If you already have a water butt attached, clean out the guttering to reduce fungal diseases in the water.
- Set up irrigation systems in the greenhouse ahead of planting so they are ready to use straight away.
- Keep a watering can full of water in the greenhouse ready to use before you dash to work. The water will also be warmer so will not shock plants when used in the morning.
- Put down capillary matting underneath pots to enable plants to soak up more water during the day.

Ventilate

Although it is important to increase humidity, a humid atmosphere where air is not moving can encourage fungal infections.

Overly high temperatures in greenhouses can also harm plants. So on warm, sunny days open all vents and leave greenhouse doors open to allow the movement of fresh air between plants. Don't forget to close them each evening to protect your plants.

Get organised

Being organised in the greenhouse will make life easier – and more productive. Keep pots, trays and tools clean and tidy. Place plants into rows so it is easier to water and identify problems that might arise with plants.

When plants are all jumbled about, problems with pests and diseases can easily be missed, and under- and over-watering can occur.

Soil borders

If you have a border in your greenhouse, reduce the build-up of soil-borne diseases by replacing the top layer with new compost or topsoil every two to three years.

It is wise not to grow the same plant in it year-after-year, as this can increase the chance of diseases taking hold.

Feed the soil with a slow release fertiliser, such as chicken manure pellets or a soil improver.

Spreading coarse gravel or grit around plants, about 2in(5cm) thick, is an effective way of slowing down the growth of weeds around the base.

WEED CONTROL

You don't need to use chemicals to control weeds in the garden.

A weed is just a plant in the wrong place, but using herbicides to get rid of them can be expensive, and may cause damage to surrounding plants.

Although we see weeds as the bad guys, it's worth having a small area where they can grow, to help wildlife.

The most important thing is to keep on top of weeds by tackling them on a regular basis – little and often is the key. Why not break the garden into sections and focus on each part over a few days?

Annual weeds are the easiest to control as they live for only a year, but they can set seed and spread rapidly. Perennial weeds tend to be deep rooted and come back year after year. Some have more than one life cycle, growing all year round. Here are some ideas to help you get rid of weeds without using chemicals in the garden.

QUICK TIP

Keep the blades on garden hoes in good working order by using a sharpening block – at any time of year.

Using flame guns

You could argue that the use of paraffin in flame guns is not an organic control. But it is an effective way of getting rid of tough perennial weeds in paving slabs and driveways, without using herbicides.

Only use on windless days and on weeds that are dry.

Hoeing

Hoeing works extremely well to kill most weed seedlings between plants in beds and borders.

Hoe on dry, sunny days with little wind, so seeds from cut weeds do not spread. The sun will also dry out any weeds on the surface before they can re-root.

Mulching

Use bark chips around plants and trees to smother weeds and slow down their growth. It will also make them easier to pull out if they do appear.

When laying mulch, leave a gap around plant stems to avoid rotting. Add the mulch to a depth of about 4in (10cm) and keep it topped up throughout the year.

Root barriers

These are placed in the soil to prevent the spread of vigorous invasive plants such as bamboo and Japanese knotweed. They can be made from iron sheets, thick plastic, old paving slabs or a toughed fabric.

Weed tools

There are many lawn weeding tools on the market.

Trowels are ideal for tackling weeds with long tap roots, and use a 'weed knife' for those in path edging.

Weed membranes

Weed membranes can be used in beds, borders and under gravel or bark chippings on garden paths.

If using in flower borders, lay the membrane just beneath the soil surface, then cut holes in it for planting. Place the membrane back around the plant and ensure it is covered with soil or bark chippings.

THE ART OF COMPOSTING

Making good compost goes a long way to making you a good gardener.

The old adage "it's all in the soil" is of course true. Create good soil and your plants will not just grow – they'll thrive.

And fundamental to this is the goodness one puts into the soil – that is, well-rotted organic matter. If you own a stable of horses then you'll never be short of material for mulching and digging-in. But most of us don't, so we must make our own organic matter. That is, compost!

Here are the five 'golden rules' of composting. Combine these with an avoidance of cooked food products (which can encourage rats), and you will be able to create lovely dark, crumbly, sweet-smelling compost.

As well as soft garden rubbish (annual weeds, fallen leaves and lawn mowings) you can and should add fruit skins and peelings from the kitchen. If your compost heap is open, as opposed to an enclosed compost bin or container, then you should water it occasionally with a hose. In this case it is also a good idea to cover it with black plastic sheeting that has small holes, to keep the heap moist.

Chop things up for faster compost

You can actually include any natural materials in your compost heap, such as unprinted paper, cotton or woollen fabric, but they should be torn up into smaller pieces first so they rot down quickly.

In fact this also applies to slightly woody plant material (such as dried dahlia, chrysanth and other perennial stems). Shredded pieces are ideal, but if you don't have a shredder then cut them up into 1-2in (2.5-5cm) long sections, before placing on the heap.

Turning compost

As well as the ingredients, and plenty of moisture, a compost heap needs oxygen. Depending on the material being put into it, an enclosed heap particularly, can often suffer from a lack of oxygen. Rectify this by forking, and turning the compost within the structure. Even better, have two compost bins. When the first becomes full, turn it out into the second. This will incorporate oxygen into the mixture, enabling it to rot down faster.

Avoiding thick layers of material

Finally, be careful not to put too much of any one thing onto the compost heap at the same time. It is crucial that the heap has a good mixture of material.

'Diversity' in the heap is better for creatures (worms, ants, woodlice, etc) that are essential to the rotting process. Most poignantly, avoid thick layers of grass clippings as these tend to turn into an anaerobic stinky mush, rather than crumbly compost. Keep grass layers to 2in (5cm) or less.

Using compost activator

Sometimes, material does not appear to rot down. If analysed there is almost always a reason why this happens – too dry, too woody, cool temperatures and so on.

You can do one of two things. Either add a couple of shovels of good garden soil (which contains bacteria that will help decomposition), or add a handful of compost activator to the heap. The latter is better than the former, as garden soil invariably contains weed seedlings.

NOTES:

Express

PROJECTS

DIY PLANT SUPPORTS

You needn't splash out on costly items to keep borders looking good, try these DIY tips for size.

The appearance of many border plants can be greatly improved with the addition of stakes and supports to protect them against wind damage or prevent them from flopping under their own weight.

For the most natural look, the key thing to remember when supporting any plant, be it climber, tall annual or weighty perennial, is to get things in place before they are needed, early in the season. If you leave it until later in the season when plants are clearly in need of help, you risk causing further damage to them and neighbouring plants, and bringing an unnatural 'manipulated' look to the plant.

When setting supports around border plants, give them space to grow – don't hem them in – as the plant grows and leans outward it will be loosely held up rather than squeezed in place.

Supports can be costly, but get a little creative and you can make your own at a fraction of the cost, either by using materials that are already lying around the garden or stored in the shed, or by picking up some cheap materials at the garden centre or DIY store.

QUICK TIP

Dip the bottom ends of wooden supports in wood preservative to prolong their use in the garden.

RECYCLE OLD HANGING BASKETS

Remove the hanging chains from the basket and turn it upside down and place over border plants.

For short, yet unruly plants, no further alterations are needed. If you want to use the basket to support a taller plant, cut three or four pieces of cane to the desired length and wire them to the basket to form legs.

Set over a plant before growth takes off and shoots will grow up through the basket wire and held in place during blustery weather.

STEP BY STEP DIY steel rod supports

1. Find the centre of the rod and wrap this around a circular object to form a hoop – a large plant pot, bin or water butt is ideal for this.

2. Sandwich the hoop between two planks then pull the rod ends up at a right angle to form the legs. It's as simple as that! Now insert into soil around your plants.

NOTES:

This bamboo support is great for mid-height border plants and is simply inserted into the soil over your chosen plants. Cut bamboo canes or similar into sections and wire together. You will need: 2 x 20in (50cm), 4 x 18in (45cm) and 2 x 28in (70cm) poles.

STEP BY STEP Bamboo grid supports

1.

Form a cross with the 20in (50cm) lengths, binding with garden wire in the centre.

2.

Form a square with the four 18in (45cm) lengths and wire together at the corners.

3.

Lay the bamboo cross centrally on top of the square and wire both parts together.

4.

Use the two 28in (70cm) lengths to create legs on opposite corners.

NATURAL PLANT SUPPORTS

A bundle of thin decorative stems cut from the garden or sourced from a craft supplier allows you to get truly creative with your plant supports. Thin, pliable stems taken from birch, willow, cornus and hazel work well for this. Use four or five thicker stems to make a wigwam, tying the tops together with twine or wire.

Create tiers up the frame with twisted bundles of thinner stems, weaving in and out of the wigwam frame. If you've got the skills, no wire is needed, but if you struggle to keep things in place use twine or wire to keep things tied in. Smaller twigs with lots of side shoots can be inserted around the base to offer support for early young shoots to clamber through.

ONE FOR THE VEG PATCH

Bamboo is so versatile and comes in a wide range of lengths, making it a suitable support option for a wide range of vegetable crops – from towering runner beans to floppy-stemmed broad beans.

Peas and mange-tout require a mid-height frame of around 4ft (1.2m) to support their shoots and developing pods.

One row of canes is angled in one direction, and a second is set in the opposite direction and wired together where they meet. Two cross poles toughen the design.

THE CHEAT'S ROCKERY

Take the easy route to adding an alpine amphitheatre to the garden.

A true rockery would see much larger stones dug into a 'hillside', sloped backwards to look like a natural rocky outcrop, creating small planting pockets in which to set a collection of alpines.

Without a slope to work with, nor the strength to lift large boulders into place, use this technique to create passable rockery displays. It allows the use of smaller stones that you can lift on your own, and helps bring costs right down. It's a quick job too. Have all the ingredients ready to hand and it won't take more than a few hours to get the look in your garden.

1.

Use up left over building bricks or rubble to create contours. Infill gaps with garden soil and cover with upturned turf.

QUICK TIP

If you can stand the wait, buy rocks now but let them weather in the garden for a year or so before use.

2.

Play with the positioning of your stones, aiming to create natural-looking rocky striations across the display.

3.

Most alpines are shallow rooting. Fill up deep gaps with gravel so you only need to lay 4-6in (10-15cm) of top soil.

4.

Alpines like a low nutrient, free-draining soil. Gather your chosen alpines. Before committing to planting them, set them out on the rockery to visualise your scheme.

5.

Set each plant in place, keeping the rootball slightly raised above surrounding soil. Set some grit/gravel around the base.

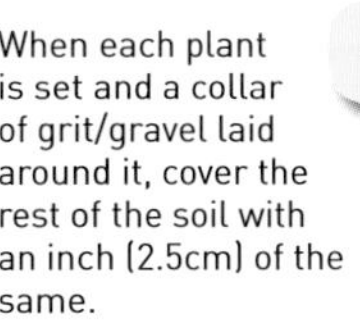

6.

When each plant is set and a collar of grit/gravel laid around it, cover the rest of the soil with an inch (2.5cm) of the same.

THE CHEAT'S ROCKERY

7.

Use a soft brush to sweep away displaced grit/gravel from the rocks and tidy the general appearance of the display.

8.

Water your new rockery. Not only will this help settle the plants, it will also wash the grit to reveal its true colour.

BBQ AND OVEN

Create a wonderful outdoor kitchen without the price tag that usually comes with it.

EASY-SOW SEEDS MATS

Bricks have so many uses in the garden, but it pays to wear a thick pair of gloves when handling them.

Usually you can only easily carry one brick at a time in each hand, unless you have someone to stack them in your hands – but then how do you set them down again once on site!?

Rather than to-ing and fro-ing for bricks during the build, spend time stacking the bricks in small piles around the build area. Instead of carrying two at a time, think about using buckets to ferry the bricks.

For a quick build, leave staggered edges to the front of the barbecue, or you could take more time and chop bricks in half using a bolster chisel and mallet.

QUICK TIP

Never lean on an unmortared brick BBQ and keep party revellers and children away from it when in use!

If you want to set your bricks in place with mortar to make your BBQ a permanent feature, use a mix of one part cement to four parts sand.

GET SET FOR SIZZLING IN SIX SIMPLE STEPS

1.

Lay out the first course of bricks four along the back and two for each side. Use a builder's set square or another brick on the inner corners to ensure all is square.

Repeat the courses, staggering the joins to add strength to the design.

2.

At the tenth course you need to lay the side bricks across the course below in order to create a lip which will hold the oven in place.

This will disrupt the staggered brickwork for a course or two, but does not significantly weaken the structure.

3.

The oven is then set in place. Once sat on the supporting bricks, stand back to check positioning. Slight adjustments to the supporting bricks below may be needed to ensure the oven is sitting centrally. The coal tray is then simply sat on top of the oven.

4.

Add two more courses of bricks and then sandwich the rack holders between them. With no mortar being used, you might have to bend these slightly for a snug fit – easily done with some pliers. Add two more courses to finish.

5.

All set for cooking! Check that the grill sits well on the holders and that the oven can open and close without obstruction. Before things heat up, add a layer of aluminium foil to the floor of the oven to make cleaning easier.

6.

For no-fail fire starting, without need for lighter fluid or blocks, invest in a BBQ fire starter. A match and newspaper is all you'll need. When the coals glow, simply pour into the tray.

Protection from the rain

You don't want your new garden oven to fill with rain water and turn rusty!

Many BBQ covers are available, but you can use a small tarpaulin. Corner ties are secured on bricks at the front, and the top's held in place with two bricks.

FUEL Express
Lumpwood
CHARCOAL
3Kg

GET COOKING

When using a fire starter the coals are ready for cooking as soon as they are poured into the tray, but it will take a while for the oven below to heat up. Avoid opening the oven too often as the heat will escape quickly. You can test it with a pizza and some jacket potatoes. Jackets can take a while, so start them off in the microwave and use the oven to crisp them up. Pizza can be ready in 10 minutes.

To prevent the BBQ meat from sticking to the grill, use non-stick BBQ spray, applied to the grill away from the hot coals before cooking. When it comes to kebabs – meat or veggie – use metal skewers as they conduct heat, helping to cook through the middle. Also, they don't catch fire like wooden skewers can!

NOTES:

SIMPLE PATHWAYS

Some easy paving ideas, perfect for a short project.

Setting out pathways needn't be a complicated or heavy job. Before you think about calling in a landscaper, look at some of the more simple ways of linking up parts of the garden and providing a stable walking surface.

Stick with gravel, wood chip or rubber chip and the task is simple – create a retaining edge, lay weed fabric and spread your chippings.

STEP BY STEP Put a spring in your step with a rubber pathway

Install retaining edges. You can use mortared bricks. A quicker, cheaper, option is to stake wooden planks in place. Leave time between the edging and the surface laying for the soil to compact, before skimming it level with a shovel.

Free-draining surfaces are prone to weed problems. Prevent establishment by laying weed fabric over the surface. Keep in place with purpose-made plastic pegs. It is easier to lay sections rather than one continuous strip.

Cover the area to a minimum of 1½ in (4cm) with rubber chippings. Rake it out to level. Unlike other chipping, you can't compact it into place with the back of a rake.

WHY CHOOSE RUBBER CHIPPINGS?

- Weighs just 10kg compared to 25kg for an equivalent bag of gravel.
- Bags are easier to lift and carry onto site.
- Does not compact.
- Discourages cats and dogs.
- Dries quickly after rain.
- Does not change colour when wet.
- Colour stays – does not fade and should look good for at least 10 years.
- Good for the environment (it's asustainable, recycled product).

SIMPLE PATHWAYS

STEP BY STEP Simple stepping stones for lawns

1.

Mow the lawn, then lay out your stepping stones on the surface. Space them out so that the person in the household with the smallest stride can comfortably use them. An old bread knife makes a great cutting tool.

2.

Having cut around each stone, remove them from the area and lift the squares of turf below with a trowel. Scratch over the soil below to level surface, then apply a layer of sand for the stones to sit on.

3.

Adjust the height so the stones sit slightly lower than the turf, then your mower will pass over easily when cutting. Use a brush to push some excavated soil in the gaps around the stones. You could also mix grass seed with the soil.

NOTES:

SMARTENING CONCRETE SURFACES WITH BRICKWORK

1. Mix mortar in batches so it does not start to set before you use it all. A good idea is to mix on a piece of board, or in an old bin to reduce the mess. Using a drill paddle makes mixing easier.

2. Lay 1in (2.5cm) of mortar over an area of around 4x4ft (1.2x1.2m). Lay your bricks, tapping them down with a rubber mallet. Check the surface with a spirit level.

3. Allow the mortar to set over night – if rain looks likely cover with a plastic sheet. The following day add your grout, either a wet or dry cement mix, or a dry filler of gravel as used here.

Simple ideas for brickwork designs

Basket weave

Running bond (along the path)

Herringbone

Running bond (across the path)

SHEDS FOR STORAGE

Two coats of paint and a nifty trick with the window turns this every-day shed into a charming garden feature while offering good storage.

Every garden should have one.

You can opt for high-end design when choosing a shed, ending up with something akin to a Swiss chalet or woodland log cabin, but boil things down, and most of us are really only after a secure weather-proof storage space for all our tools and sundries. Bear this in mind and a new shed needn't cost you the earth.

A shed will ensure all your tools and products stay dry over winter. Down-sizing allows for a bit of storage space at the back and side for weatherproof pots and bits of timber, etc.

Sheds come flat packed (with many suppliers offering a build service). Each make and model will be supplied with their own assembly instructions. Here are some tips for you to end up with a fine looking shed that will enhance your garden as well as provideing essential storage.

3 TIPS FOR FLOORS AND BASES

1. Sleepers make a sturdy, durable base and allow air flow under the shed. Dig out the area, firm the soil, set the sleepers and check levels.

2. Make shed floors easier to clean and more attractive with lino offcuts. These can be picked up cheaply from carpet and flooring stores.

3. Create extra head height by sandwiching a decking board frame between the floor and walls, fixing with L brackets.

Shiplap or overlap?

You have two options when it comes to build finish. An overlap (or featherboard) finish is the cheapest option, as the wood is rougher and the factory build is less involved (shown right).

Shiplap offers a finer finish. The wood is planed smooth and is interlocking, leading to better insulation and a sturdier looking shed (shown left).

The build

Assembly of most standard sheds is pretty straight forward. Once a side panel is screwed to the back panel it becomes self-supporting (just watch out for strong gusts of wind!).

If you want to collect rain water from the roof but want to squeeze your shed into a tight spot, add guttering to the side panels before setting them in place.

It is often easier to lay the front panel down to screw the doors in place, rather than try to support the weight of the doors while hanging them to the finished shed.

Roofing

Felt is the standard option for weatherproofing shed roofs and this is generally supplied as part of the kit. An average-sized shed will require three strips. Secure the lower two strips first. Then overlap the third across the apex of the roof and tack down over the others, so rain water runs over the seams rather than into them. Use sealant around tacks to finish.

Inside

It pays to be well organised inside the shed. The more shelving, tool racks, hooks etc the better. Think about using old house furniture too – drawer units, cupboards etc.

Sturdy shopping bags make good storage for smaller items.

Shed security

Despite the padlock, a standard bolt like this can simply be unscrewed by a determined thief.

Better to use a hasp and staple design. Once padlocked, the screws are hidden from view.

If you have been targeted by shed thieves in the past or if it is a problem in your area, something more heavy duty is called for. A steel security bar will keep your shed contents safe and secure.

Windows

Sheds can be dark and dingy places and a window will go a long way to alleviate this. However a window will reduce the amount of shelving you can install inside, so you'll need to weigh your options.

Sheds can be untidy places too. To prevent contents being seen from the garden you can coat the pane with etching spray, which will still let in light, or cover it with a decorative static clingfilm. These also offer added security as would-be thieves won't know what's hidden inside.

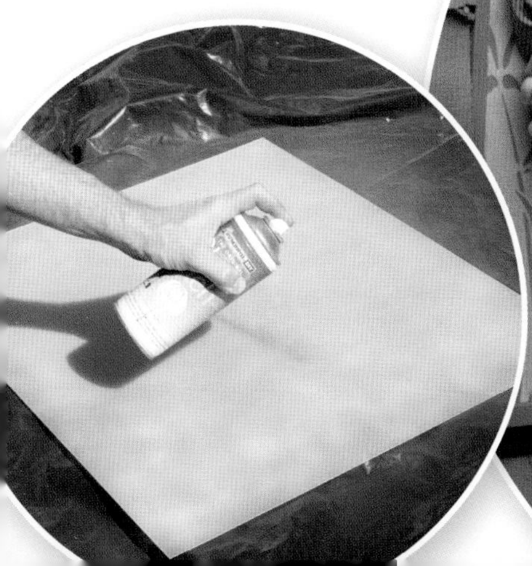

PLANTING A TIERED GARDEN

Plant up a tiered border, starting with tall plants.

Autumn is the season to set out hardy plants, including perennials. Planting now gives roots time to settle in and grow so they can support strong new growth in the spring.

A border that is 4ft (1.2m) or more from front to back, gives you the opportunity to put in layers of plants – tallest at the back, the medium-sized plants in the middle, and short or low ones at the front.

Don't be too precise about height levels – mix things up a bit for variety, nudging one or two taller plants forward. Add evergreens for winter interest.

Add some evergreens to provide winter structure.

STEP BY STEP Planting at the back of a border

Dig the area, and remove all weeds. Firm soil by treading, and rake it. Add a phosphate fertiliser such as bonemeal to boost root growth.

Dig a hole a bit bigger than the pot. Remove pot and set plant in the hole so the compost surface is level with soil.

Firm the plant in position tucking soil tightly around the roots. Water it in, and tidy up the soil surrounding it to remove footprints.

4-7ft (1.2-2.1m) tall

- *Alcea* (hollyhock)
- *Echinops ritro* 'Taplow Blue'
- *Campanula latifolia*
- *Crocosmia* 'Lucifer'
- *Helenium* 'Chipperfield Orange'
- *Ligularia przewalskii* 'The Rocket'
- *Helianthus maximum*

Wikimedia/Tim Green

8-10ft (1.5-3m) tall

- *Cortaderia selloana*
- *Macleaya cordata*
- *Delphinium elatum* hybrids
- *Eupatorium purpureum*
- *Thalictrum flavum subsp. glaucum*
- *Helianthus* 'Giant Single' (sunflower)
- *Eremurus robustus*

Wikimedia

NOTES: